VOLUME THREE

THE

R·U·L·E·S

ENGAGEMENT

SATANIC WEAPONS EXPOSED

DR. N. CINDY TRIMM

CREATION HOUSE
A STRANG COMPANY

RULES OF ENGAGEMENT, VOL. 3
SATANIC WEAPONS EXPOSED
by Dr. N. Cindy Trimm
Published by Creation House
A Strang Company
600 Rinehart Road
Lake Mary, Florida 32746
www.creationhouse.com

Unless otherwise noted, all Scripture quotations are from the King James Version of the Bible.

Scripture quotations marked NIV are from the Holy Bible, New International Version. Copyright 1973, 1978, 1984, International Bible Society. Used by permission.

Scripture quotations marked MSG are from *The Message: The Bible in Contemporary English*, copyright 1993, 1994, 1995, 1996, 2000, 2001, 2002. Used by permission of Nav-Press Publishing Group.

Cover design by Terry Clifton

Library of Congress Control Number: 2005927879
International Standard Book Number: 1-59185-823-2

Second Edition

06 07 08 09 10 — 10 9 8 7 6 5 4 3 2
Printed in the United States of America

Contents

Introduction

WHEN THE LORD initially introduced me to the concepts of intrinsic and extrinsic weapons, they were merely revelational words that were downloaded into my conscious mind by the Holy Spirit as He trained me in the art of strategic prayer and spiritual warfare. I employed these terms in my prayer vocabulary and later added them as one of the warfare declarations in the first volume of The Rules of Engagement Series. A few months after the initial revelation, my spirit really grasped the true meaning of these terms, and the Holy Spirit once again began to reveal to me how potent the scriptural declaration "no weapon formed against me shall prosper," really was. My paradigm instantly shifted from the mere utterance of a phrase that provided me with an intellectually conceptualized arsenal, and the understanding of how the wiles of the devil are actually executed, to an understanding of how powerful intrinsic and extrinsic satanic weapons really were. This one declaration opened my eyes to see how covert the attack of the enemy really was in my own life. I began to make enquiries of the Lord concerning the diversity and magnitude of these weapons of mass destruction. Some of them I was aware of and others I was not. I want to ask you two questions: Has any one ever quoted to you the scripture taken from Isaiah 54:17, "No weapon forged against you will prevail" (NIV)? Has anyone ever explained to you what the weapons were? At this very moment, I am sitting in my hotel room in London editing this book. It is 5:21 a.m. and I feel anointed by the Father to dialogue with you concerning the content of this book. It is more than just an author's revelation of weapons that are formed against saints. To me it is a book written so that you can both discern and identify how the enemy is fighting against you, the weapon(s) he has designed for your demise, and how to successfully counteract.

This is a user-friendly book in that the definitions have been kept simple. It is written to arm you with specific insights into the actual weapons used. It is not a book that is designed to alarm, but to arm.

If a military is going to win a war, there are several important questions that must be answered:

- Who is the enemy?
- Where is the battle?
- What are his weapons?

I believe most Christians will be able to answer questions one and two. The answer to the first question is obvious. The enemy is Satan and his cohorts. Since the rebellion of Satan and one-third of the angels, this world has been in combat against demonic forces. Having elaborately established an insidious military spiritual force, Satan continues to fulfill his mission: to steal, kill, and destroy all that belongs to God and is godly. The answer to the second question is the mind. The enemy forms and forges a great variety of weapons. Some are more apparent then others, such as abuse and afflictions. Others are not as evident, such as the spirit of indifference and frustration.

The Book of Genesis is full of examples of how the enemy forms and utilizes these weapons. For example in Genesis 2:15, God instructs Adam to dress and keep the Garden of Eden. According to *Strong's Dictionary of Hebrew and Greek Words*, the word *dress* comes from the Hebrew word *abad* and is translated, "to administrate, to implement or execute as in the ingenious working of an idea so as to cause something to come to pass by tilling, plowing, and cultivating." The word *dress* is also translated as *worship*. Adam's work was his worship. The word *keep* comes from the Hebrew word *shamar*, which is translated "to hedge about, to guard, to protect, and to attend to." It also carries the connotations "to beware, to be circumspect, to take heed to, to watch (as in intercession and prayer), and to save oneself." Inherent in his divine assignment was the anointing to accomplish the instructions given. It also gave Adam the heads-up, warning him that there was an enemy lurking about the borders of the garden: to be forewarned is to be "fore-armed." One would think Adam would remain vigilant. But Adam underestimated the enemy. Yes, he was anointed; yes, he maintained continuous communication with God; yes, he was fulfilling his assignment. But by the time he recognized the surreptitious seduction of the enemy, the catastrophe had already occurred. We see the same kind of divine warning given to Cain:

And the LORD said unto Cain, Why art thou wroth? and why is thy countenance fallen? If thou doest well, shalt thou not be accepted? and if thou doest not well, sin lieth at the door. And unto thee shall be his desire, and thou shalt rule over him.

—GENESIS 4:6–7

The enemy is portrayed as a crouching lion waiting for the most opportune moment to pounce upon its unsuspecting prey. First Peter 5:8 exhorts you to "be sober, be vigilant; because your adversary the devil, as a roaring lion, walketh about, seeking whom he may devour." The word *may* is the key word in this passage. It says to me that Satan cannot devour everyone. He cannot devour you if you are aware of his tactics and strategies because the weapons you fight with are far greater than his. According to 2 Corinthians 10:4–5, "The weapons of our warfare are not carnal, but mighty through God to the pulling down of strong holds; Casting down imaginations, and every high thing that exalteth itself against the knowledge of God, and bringing into captivity every thought to the obedience of Christ." From this scripture alone we can conclude that the weapons the enemy uses against us are primarily carnal in nature: ones that involve the mind, will, and emotions.

In order to defend against Satan and his deceptive attacks, we must first understand what we are defending against. Imagine, for example, that you are a general with tens of thousands of soldiers and weapons at your command. The battlefield is pitch black—and as events would have it, you don't at this moment have night-vision goggles and equipment. You know out there somewhere is another general with his battalions. But you don't know how many soldiers he has on the battlefield. You don't know if your soldiers will be facing tanks, cannon, planes, or missiles.

You don't know whether the terrain is mountainous or wet and swampy. Can you plan a battle effectively? Absolutely not! Everything would be guesswork; both you and your soldiers would be at a disadvantage and in greater danger of being killed. Our general, the Lord Jesus Christ, is not an uninformed general. He knows the enemy, his arsenal, and the terrain. The battlefield is the mind, the weapons... well, you are about to discover.

As the enemy wages war against you, remember— you are fighting *the good fight of faith*. Your concentration should not merely rest upon what happens to you, but also what is happening in you and your response to what happens to you. According to Daniel 7:25–27, Satan wants to cause you to become fatigued and give up. He wants to wear you out, causing you to become battle-fatigued and to give in. But don't you give up; don't give in. The same text indicates that we not only prevail, we also overcome every attack. Remember, the flip side of victory is warfare, and the flip side of warfare, victory. Either way, you win.

So, my brothers and sisters, "Gird up the loins of your mind, be sober, and hope to the end" (1 Pet. 1:13). Do not give up in this battle, and do not let the enemy wear you down. "Therefore, my beloved brethren, be ye stedfast, unmoveable, always abounding in the work of the Lord, forasmuch as ye know that your labour is not in vain in the Lord" (1 Cor. 15:58). Therefore, since it is common knowledge that the enemy lurks about seeking whom he *may* devour (emphasis on *may*, not *devour*), don't let him devour you.

If he has targeted you during this season, he will be very definite about his attack. Just like any natural army he even has a reconnaissance team. They are known as familiar spirits. They are responsible for surveillance and informing Satan of areas of weakness and probable strategies that can be employed to sabotage the fulfillment of purpose and destiny. It is encouraging to know that, like Job, we are able to be protected and even hidden behind prayer shields, spiritual hedges, and firewalls. As a believer you are responsible for making sure that there are no perforations in your spiritual hedge or cracks in your firewalls. Satan is always looking for a way to penetrate the life of an unsuspecting prey. An example of this is found in the Book of Job:

> Now there was a day when the sons of God came to present themselves before the Lord, and Satan came also among them. And the Lord said unto Satan, Whence comest thou? Then Satan answered the Lord, and said, From going to and fro in the earth, and from walking up and down in it. And the Lord said unto Satan, Hast thou considered my servant Job, that there is none like him in the earth, a perfect and an upright man, one that feareth God, and escheweth evil? Then Satan answered the Lord, and said, Doth Job fear God for nought? Hast not thou made an hedge about him, and about his house, and about all that he hath on every side? thou hast blessed the work of his hands, and his substance is increased in the land.
>
> —Job 1:6–10

When Satan initially targeted Job, he complained to God that there was a hedge built around him. It was not until that hedge was removed that Satan could attack. If you sense that Satan is attacking you and perhaps your hedge of protection has been compromised, I encourage you to acquire a copy of my book, *The Rules of Engagement, Vol 1.* Pray the prayer, decreeing and declaring that a prayer shield, the anointing, and blood form your hedge of protection, with angels marshalling the boundaries of your property and personage. Ask God to supernaturally reinforce and thicken your hedge of protection. When you fight, fight under the covering and in the strength of the Lord. Ensure you are wearing your protective spiritual armor. Remember, Psalm 91:1 speaks of divine covering, while Ephesians 6:10–11 outlines your protective armor.

Many weapons the enemy uses against you can often go undetected because, as Christians, we are deceived into believing that his weapons do not include obvious things such as thoughts and emotions. These weapons are intrinsic in nature. Emotions are the perfect weapon because the enemy can convince you that they are only "feelings." I guess the natural question in response to this statement is, "How can the enemy use my emotions as an intrinsic weapon?" Emotions can be used to do harm to your physical body. They can do more harm than you can ever imagine. Take bitterness, for instance. It has been proven to be a contributing factor to arthritic conditions. Longstanding, unresolved issues are said to be contributing factors to high blood pressure. Be careful. Do not accept every emotion or feeling as yours because some of those feelings may have been projected onto you.

This book is designed to expose weapons that Satan successfully uses to affect the quality of our lives. Many of these weapons are in fact spirits that are sent to give diabolical counsel to the mind. They speak in first person, singular, using the word "I," as in "I feel sick," "I feel mad," or "I am irritated," so that you feel as if these are your thoughts or feelings. I remember returning home one night after ministry. I sat on the edge of my bed and all of a sudden "I" felt sad. Thoughts started racing through my mind, and my internal dialogue was incredibly and unusually negative. Since I am a basically positive person, initially I dismissed it as fatigue. However, the thoughts became so overpowering that I began to entertain them as if they were mine. I wanted to leave the ministry, forget about everything and everyone. Then the Holy Spirit rose up in me and instructed me to fight against the thoughts. I took on a posture of prayer and spiritual warfare, commanding the spirit to go. After binding and loosing and releasing the spirit from its assignment, I heard a "woosh" sound and felt a presence leave my bedroom through the window. The thoughts and emotions I claimed as mine were really spirits of depression, abortion (trying to abort my ministry), and frustration. This is how deceptive the weapons of the enemy are. Remember: when spirits come, they come to give diabolical counsel to your mind because this level of warfare is spiritual, not carnal. Therefore, when you engage in warfare at this level, you must remember that according to 1 Corinthians 10:3–6, every thought must be taken captive by the lordship of Christ and His Word. This is what happened to Jesus in the wilderness. The voice of the enemy spoke to Him on three occasions. You have to understand that the conversation was not verbal, as the following text describes:

> Then was Jesus led up of the Spirit into the wilderness to be tempted of the devil. And when he had fasted forty days and forty nights, he was afterward an hungred. And when the tempter came to him, he said, If thou be the Son of God, command that these stones be made bread. But he answered and said, It is written, Man shall not

live by bread alone, but by every word that proceedeth out of the mouth of God. Then the devil taketh him up into the holy city, and setteth him on a pinnacle of the temple, and saith unto him, If thou be the Son of God, cast thyself down: for it is written, He shall give his angels charge concerning thee: and in their hands they shall bear thee up, lest at any time thou dash thy foot against a stone. Jesus said unto him, It is written again, Thou shalt not tempt the Lord thy God. Again, the devil taketh him up into an exceeding high mountain, and sheweth him all the kingdoms of the world, and the glory of them; and saith unto him, All these things will I give thee, if thou wilt fall down and worship me. Then saith Jesus unto him, Get thee hence, Satan: for it is written, Thou shalt worship the Lord thy God, and him only shalt thou serve. Then the devil leaveth him, and, behold, angels came and ministered unto him.

—MATTHEW 4:1–11

Notice Jesus fought with the Word of the Lord and brought His thoughts under its authority. You must do the same. The devil was after Jesus' authority and dominion in the earth-realm. He is after yours. Do not give it away. You must fight every thought that does not align itself with the Word of God and fight with the God's Word. Cast the thoughts down and bring them under the authority of the Word and under the Lordship of Christ.

This book gives a list of intrinsic (internal), extrinsic (external), and esoteric (obscure/hidden) weapons the enemy could possibly employ in his attack against you. For ease of reference, weapons have been alphabetized. Scripture references are given to provide further biblical insight and revelation of how the enemy utilizes these weapons. Read each section carefully and prayerfully. Remain vigilant. Rest assured that although the enemy will attempt to exact himself upon you, you can go into every battle armed with the knowledge of 2 Corinthians 2:14, "God...always causeth us to triumph in Christ, and maketh manifest the savour of his knowledge by us in every place." Indeed, "No weapon that is formed against thee shall prosper" (Isa. 54:17).

As you begin to receive revelation from this book, I pray that as Adam was ushered into the Garden of Eden, a kind of wealthy place, that according to Psalm 66:12 God will also usher you into your wealthy place. I decree and declare that areas the enemy has hitherto gained a stronghold in, God will bring complete victory. May your mind become like the Garden of Eden prior to the fall—a place of peace and serenity, saturated by the presence of God.

If you have suffered any loss, I also decree and declare that the anointing of Job for restoration be released upon you. Things that the enemy stole, destroyed, or undermined are being restored to you double-fold. What a wonderful encouragement the following scripture has been to me, and I pray that it will encourage you:

And the LORD turned the captivity of Job, when he prayed for his friends: also the LORD gave Job twice as much as he had before. Then came there unto him all his brethren, and all his sisters, and all they that had been of his acquaintance before, and did eat bread with him in his house: and they bemoaned him, and comforted him over all the evil that the LORD had brought upon him: every man also gave him a piece of money, and every one an earring of gold. So the LORD blessed the latter end of Job more than his beginning: for he had fourteen thousand sheep, and six thousand camels, and a thousand yoke of oxen, and a thousand she asses. He had also seven sons and three daughters.

—Job 42:10–13

I exhort you to:

Rejoice in the Lord your God: for he hath given you the former rain moderately, and he will cause to come down for you the rain, the former rain, and the latter rain in the first month. And the floors shall be full of wheat, and the fats shall overflow with wine and oil. And I will restore to you the years that the locust hath eaten, the cankerworm, and the caterpillar, and the palmerworm, my great army which I sent among you. And ye shall eat in plenty, and be satisfied, and praise the name of the Lord your God, that hath dealt wondrously with you: and my people shall never be ashamed.

—Joel 2:23–26

Abandonment

When a person withdraws their presence and support from another person or organization, and reneges on their duty, responsibility, and obligation, and betrays covenant or commitment, this is called abandonment. The enemy seduces people, particularly those who play a key role in the life of another person or organization's development and progress, to renege on commitments and contracts, and to walk away from relationships and responsibilities. This act of abdication has the power to cause great emotional pain, financial hardship, spiritual misalignment, organizational chaos, and confusion in the abandoned. Abandonment can be both physical and emotional. Legally, abandonment is defined as the forsaking of a station involving public or social duties without justification or reason, and with the intention of not returning. In military law, it is defined as the failure to arrive at a place of duty without leave; in time of war, especially in the face of the enemy. In maritime law, a seaman who abandons a ship without leave is rendered liable to damages and forfeits the wages he has already earned. In family law, abandonment is described as the willful desertion by one spouse in a marriage, without the consent of the other. The refusal to renew cohabitation without justification is also considered desertion, and in some instances the mere abstinence from sexual intercourse or the refusal by a husband to support his wife has been regarded as abandonment particularly if he has the means to support her. With regard to parenting issues, notwithstanding the obvious domestic absence of a parent constituting abandonment, there is also the less then obvious: emotional/psychological abandonment. Issues arising from abandonment, such as the inability to trust, manipulation, shame, fear of rejection, loneliness, suspicion, addictions, codependency, and a host of other maladaptive sets of behavior interferes with the victim's ability to foster future healthy and loving relationships. In the case of an organization, sometimes the timing of the occurrence can set that organization back for months or years, or sabotage it beyond its ability to survive. If you or any organization you are a part of have experienced the effect of this weapon, it is my prayer that God strengthens you, infuses life back into the organization, and sends committed individuals to replace the perpetrator(s). I also pray that God will be with you as He heals you of past experiences and protects you from future occurrences.

Paul experienced ministerial abandonment, but God provided for him three individuals—Timothy, Mark, and Luke—to encourage and refresh him during his season of testing:

> Do thy diligence to come shortly unto me: For Demas hath forsaken me, having loved this present world, and is departed unto Thessalonica; Crescens to Galatia, Titus unto Dalmatia. Only Luke is with me. Take Mark, and bring him with thee: for he is profitable to me for the ministry. And Tychicus have I sent to Ephesus. The cloke that I left at Troas with Carpus, when thou comest, bring with thee, and the books, but especially the parchments. Alexander the coppersmith did me much evil: the Lord reward him according to his works: Of whom be thou ware also; for he hath greatly withstood our words. At my first answer no man stood with me, but all men forsook me: I pray God that it may not be laid to

their charge. Notwithstanding the Lord stood with me, and strengthened me; that by me the preaching might be fully known, and that all the Gentiles might hear: and I was delivered out of the mouth of the lion. And the Lord shall deliver me from every evil work, and will preserve me unto his heavenly kingdom: to whom be glory for ever and ever. Amen.

—2 Timothy 4:9–18

Counterattack: Ask God to give you your prophetic "Timothy," "Mark," or "Luke" on whom you can depend in your time of need. Quote Psalm 27:10, "When my father [covering, anyone responsible to facilitate organizational or relational destiny] and my mother [anyone who is responsible for financial, emotional, moral support, etc.] forsake me, then the Lord will take me up."

Abortion

There are two perspectives I want to give concerning abortion. First, I offer the traditional. According to the *American Heritage Dictionary,* abortion is an induced termination of pregnancy and expulsion of an embryo or fetus. In an attempt to be a sensitive as I can in handling this subject, I do not want to come across as condemning because in Christ Jesus there is no condemnation. Once the woman/young girl consents and actually undergoes an abortion, they become both victim and perpetrator. The abortion does not merely "un-pregnant" a person, it molds both the woman and those who support it and perform it murderers. It opens the door for a spirit of death to destroy other areas of their lives, creating cycles of death that allow the enemy to access their lives to steal, kill, and destroy not only the quality of their lives, but also business ventures, relationships, and ministries while sending the spirit of death down to future generations. Long-term ramifications are mind-boggling. But thanks be to God, Romans 8:2 gives every person hope, "For the law of the Spirit of life in Christ Jesus hath made me free from the law of sin and death." The second has to do with a variety of other activities normally not associated with the aforementioned concept. These weapons are meticulously crafted to destroy an individual, organization, or any other entity's chance of maximizing potential or the fulfillment of purpose. The spirit of abortion not only affects the physical womb, but it also affects all twenty-six wombs of the spirit. This one statement implies that there are other abortive activities that the enemy is involved in. For instance, murder, accidents, premature deaths, sabotage, and less obvious activities such as laziness, gossip, fear, underbelief, and slander. Each one of these abortive activities affects one or more areas of a person's life and has the power to terminate things such as ministries, business opportunities, relationships, purpose, and potential. Abortion does not only kill a natural fetus, but also the many different blessings that heaven is pregnant with for you, your dreams and visions, plans and purpose, desires and aspirations. Many people have lost their marriages, ministries, businesses, business opportunities, or relationships because of careless vicious gossip, the defamation of their character by slanderous actions, or even the malignant carelessness associated with laziness which are all spiritual instruments of abortion. The delivered adult Hebrew slaves never made it into the Promised Land. Their entire future prosperity and life was aborted because of fear and unbelief. There is such a high level of misunderstanding when it comes to abortion that the enemy has created a stronghold in many societies through misunderstanding and miseducation of the masses. May God sustain and protect your loved ones and everything and everyone associated with you from the spirit of abortion, and break death cycles associated with it in Jesus' name.

Counterattack: Ask the Lord to forgive you and to free you from all present and future ramifications associated with an abortion or abortive activities. Renounce all satanic contracts and covenants with the spirit of death. Break soul-ties and strongholds associated with abortive activities. Bind the spirit of death and break death cycles from your life, home, business, marriage, children, and loved ones. Confess that your body is the temple of the Holy Spirit, cleansed and sanctified by the blood of Jesus Christ. Close all spiritual portals to your soul from the enemy. Establish Jehovah as the gatekeeper and doorkeeper to your soul. Build prayer hedges around your life, the life of your loved ones, business, ministry, and relationships.

Abuse

Abuse is defined as the mistreatment of something or someone.

Physical Abuse

Physical abuse is the ill treatment of another individual, child or adult, which may or may not cause injury. This includes punching, hitting, slapping, pinching, and shaking. Physical abuse can also occur when people are not provided with adequate care and support, causing them unjustifiable physical discomfort. For example, unwarranted or inappropriate restraint, forced isolation or confinement, and withholding or absence of necessary aids. Physical abuse also includes the improper administration of drugs, treatments, or medication.

Psychological Abuse

This results from being repeatedly made to feel unhappy, anxious, afraid, humiliated, or devalued by the actions, inactions, and attitudes of others. This may include:

- Humiliation—making a vulnerable adult feel ashamed of involuntary behavior, blaming a vulnerable adult for attitudes, actions, or events beyond their control, or making behavior, attainment, or physical appearance a target for ridicule.

- Intimidation—name-calling, threats, continued shouting, or use of abusive language. This also includes racist comments and deprivation of cultural identity.

Sexual Abuse

Sexual behavior that might be abusive includes acts that involve physical contact and others which do not. It includes one-off assault or sexual acts within an ongoing relationship in which either the adult's vulnerability precludes consent or the power imbalance is too great for their consent to be considered valid.

Financial or Material Abuse

People have rights enshrined in law regarding medical care, freedom of movement, speech, and association. These must be respected by any person or organization providing care. Material or legal abuse may include:

- Material exploitation—the misuse of the vulnerable person's money, property, possessions, or insurance, or blocking access to these material goods.

- Personal exploitation—denying the rights of a competent adult, for example to the right to complain, to vote, or to seek independent legal advice.

- Theft—stealing the vulnerable adult's money, property, possessions, or insurance, or extortion through threats and misappropriation.

Institutional Abuse

Institutional abuse includes the practice of an abusive regime or culture that destroys the dignity and respect to which every person is entitled. It occurs when the individual's wishes and needs are sacrificed for the smooth running of an institution, organization, or home. This may include:

- Infantilization of adults

- Denying or failing to promote people's rights

- The provision of an unsafe or unhygienic environment

- Lack of privacy

- Racial harassment

- Lack of provision for dress, diet, or religious observance.

Social Abuse

The abuse of the vulnerable person's right to social interaction and social contact. This may be intentional or unintentional and may include withdrawal from a valued activity, denial of access to community events/groups, or denied access to friends and family.

Neglect

Neglect is the deliberate withholding or unintentional failure to provide appropriate and adequate care or support necessary for the adult to carry out daily living tasks.

Discriminatory Abuse

This abuse is motivated by oppressive and discriminatory attitudes toward:

- A person's disability, including physical or learning disability, ill mental health, or sensory impairment.
- Race
- Age
- Gender
- Religion
- Cultural background
- Sexual orientation

Counterattack: Decree and declare daily Exodus 19:5. I am God's treasured possession, He will cause everything to work together for me because He loves me with an everlasting love. I release myself from being ensnared by unforgiveness and receive divine empowerment to walk away from the abuse and take control over my destiny. I decree and declare that with God all things are possible, and today, according to Philippians 3:13, I forget those things which are behind and reach forth unto those things which are before. Heal me of all hurt and pain,

"Thou art my hiding place; thou shalt preserve me from trouble; thou shalt compass me about with songs of deliverance" (Ps. 32:7).

Accident

When I talk about accidents I am not only referring to those that are seemingly caused by human error but also unexplainable events caused by forces outside of human instigation. I believe that satanic forces can instigate catastrophic events. These occurrences are abortive undertakings designed to frustrate or foil the will of God in the earth realm. The following event narrated by Luke is an example of a satanically orchestrated accident waiting to happen. The intent, it would appear, was to sabotage the mission of Jesus in the country of the Gergesenes, where therein awaited a demon-possessed individual divinely scheduled for deliverance that day. Had the enemy successfully completed this undertaking, lives would have been lost and the demoniac would have remained under the control and influence of Satan:

> Now when much time was spent, and when sailing was now dangerous, because the fast was now already past, Paul admonished them, and said unto them, Sirs, I perceive that this voyage will be with hurt and much damage, not only of the lading and ship, but also of our lives. Nevertheless the centurion believed the master and the owner of the ship, more than those things which were spoken by Paul. And because the haven was not commodious to winter in, the more part advised to depart thence also, if by any means they might attain

to Phenice, and there to winter; which is an haven of Crete, and lieth toward the south west and north west. And when the south wind blew softly, supposing that they had obtained their purpose, loosing thence, they sailed close by Crete. But not long after there arose against it a tempestuous wind, called Euroclydon. And when the ship was caught, and could not bear up into the wind, we let her drive. And running under a certain island which is called Clauda, we had much work to come by the boat: which when they had taken up, they used helps, undergirding the ship; and, fearing lest they should fall into the quicksands, strake sail, and so were driven. And we being exceedingly tossed with a tempest, the next day they lightened the ship; and the third day we cast out with our own hands the tackling of the ship. And when neither sun nor stars in many days appeared, and no small tempest lay on us, all hope that we should be saved was then taken away. But after long abstinence Paul stood forth in the midst of them, and said, Sirs, ye should have hearkened unto me, and not have loosed from Crete, and to have gained this harm and loss. And now I exhort you to be of good cheer: for there shall be no loss of any man's life among you, but of the ship. For there stood by me this night the angel of God, whose I am, and whom I serve, saying, Fear not, Paul; thou must be brought before Caesar: and, lo, God hath given thee all them that sail with thee. Wherefore, sirs, be of good cheer: for I believe God, that it shall be even as it was told me. Howbeit we must be cast upon a certain island. But when the fourteenth night was come, as we were driven up and down in Adria, about midnight the shipmen deemed that they drew near to some country; and sounded, and found it twenty fathoms: and when they had gone a little further, they sounded again, and found it fifteen fathoms. Then fearing lest we should have fallen upon rocks, they cast four anchors out of the stern, and wished for the day. And as the shipmen were about to flee out of the ship, when they had let down the boat into the sea, under colour as though they would have cast anchors out of the foreship, Paul said to the centurion and to the soldiers, Except these abide in the ship, ye cannot be saved. Then the soldiers cut off the ropes of the boat, and let her fall off. And while the day was coming on, Paul besought them all to take meat, saying, This day is the fourteenth day that ye have tarried and continued fasting, having taken nothing. Wherefore I pray you to take some meat: for this is for your health: for there shall not an hair fall from the head of any of you. And when he had thus spoken, he took bread, and gave thanks to God in presence of them all: and when he had broken it, he began to eat. Then were they all of good cheer, and they also took some meat. And we were in all in the ship two hundred threescore and sixteen souls. And when they had eaten enough, they lightened the ship, and cast out the wheat into the sea. And when it was day, they knew not the land: but they discovered a certain creek with a shore, into the which they were minded, if it were possible, to thrust in the ship. And when they had taken up the anchors, they committed themselves unto the sea, and loosed the rudder bands, and hoised up the mainsail to the wind, and made toward shore. And falling into a place where two seas met, they ran the ship aground; and the forepart stuck fast, and remained unmoveable, but the hinder part was broken with the violence of the waves. And the soldiers' counsel was to kill the prisoners, lest any of them should swim out, and escape. But the centurion, willing to save Paul, kept them from their purpose; and commanded that they which could swim should cast themselves first into the sea, and get to land: and the rest, some on boards, and some on broken pieces of the ship. And so it came to pass, that they escaped all safe to land.

—ACTS 27:9–44

Counterattack: Quote Psalm 91:9–12, "Because thou hast [I have] made the LORD, which is my refuge, even the most High, thy [my] habitation; there shall no evil befall thee [me], neither shall any plague come nigh thy [my] dwelling. For he shall give his angels charge over thee [me], to keep thee [me] in all thy ways. They shall bear thee [me] up in their hands, lest thou [I] dash thy [my] foot against a stone." Bind the spirits of inheritance and decree and declare that you are free from all accidents in Jesus' name. Come against every abortive activity and acts of sabotage in Jesus' name.

Accusation

Accusation is the act of attributing blame and wrongdoings. This is one of the enemy's weapons of choice when it comes to disturbing personal peace, undermining purpose, and destroying faith in God, particularly if the accusations are fabricated. The accuser of the brethren will not only personally accuse you, but also, like a master chess player, he uses other people as pawns to bring you to the point of hearing him declare "checkmate" and defeating you completely. Whenever you see individuals accusing one another, or you begin to accuse and point fingers, ask yourself this question: "Is the accuser of the brethren at the helm of this?" Accusations can go from one extreme to the other: the blatant, such as indictments and impeachments; and the sublime, such as insinuations and innuendos.

It pleased Darius to set over the kingdom an hundred and twenty princes, which should be over the whole kingdom; and over these three presidents; of whom Daniel was first: that the princes might give accounts unto them, and the king should have no damage. Then this Daniel was preferred above the presidents and princes, because an excellent spirit was in him; and the king thought to set him over the whole realm. Then the presidents and princes sought to find occasion against Daniel concerning the kingdom; but they could find none occasion nor fault; forasmuch as he was faithful, neither was there any error or fault found in him. Then said these men, We shall not find any occasion against this Daniel, except we find it against him concerning the law of his God. Then these presidents and princes assembled together to the king, and said thus unto him, King Darius, live for ever. All the presidents of the kingdom, the governors, and the princes, the counsellers, and the captains, have consulted together to establish a royal statute, and to make a firm decree, that whosoever shall ask a petition of any God or man for thirty days, save of thee, O king, he shall be cast into the den of lions.

—DANIEL 6:1–7

And I heard a loud voice saying in heaven, Now is come salvation, and strength, and the kingdom of our God, and the power of his Christ: for the accuser of our brethren is cast down, which accused them before our God day and night.

—REVELATION 12:10

Counterattack: Ask God to vindicate you in the name of Jesus. Decree and declare that no weapon formed against you will prosper and that every lying tongue is silenced. Come against falsehoods, slander, speculation, accusation, misrepresentation, and character assassination. Father, cause the heavens to bow down with divine judgment; cast forth lightning to scatter your accuser. Ask God to send His hand from above and rid you of them. (See Psalm 144:5–7.) Ask God to prohibit the accuser of the brethren from operating or influencing soul or mind of anyone who comes into contact with me. (See Revelation 12:10.) Decree and declare that your name is associated with integrity, holiness, righteousness, and uprightness, and that the Lord will vindicate you in due season. Maintain a posture dictated by James 4:7, "Submit yourselves therefore to God. Resist the devil, and he will flee from you."

Addictions

There are both popular and professional definitions for the word *addiction*. When a layperson attempts to define what an addiction is, usually they will describe a person who is addicted to something that creates an unhealthy habit or a social disease. According to the *American Heritage Dictionary* an addiction is a compulsive physical or psychological need for habit-forming substances, activities, or experiences. In short, it is any engagement in a compulsive behavior. All addiction includes some degree of compulsions and obsessions. Although there is still some debate about the difference between addictions, compulsions, and obsessions, basically an addiction is something which you enjoy doing, or started off enjoying and involves some degree of physical dependence. An obsession is an idea or a thought dominating a person's mind, while a compulsion is defined as an irresistible urge or a repetitive behavior (e.g. cleaning or checking something continually). An addiction is also characterized by a behavior performed in response to an obsession. Addictions can spin off into what is psychological termed as obsessive-compulsive disorders (OCD). For ease of reference, I have listed addictions under two headings:

Substance: alcohol, heroin, tobacco, solvents, cocaine, crack, cannabis, caffeine, steroids, tranquilizers, hallucinogens, amphetamines, ecstasy, painkillers, barbiturates.

Social: over-exercising, sex, sexual perversions, pornography, eating disorders (anorexia, bulimia, overeating), techno-addictions (computer games, cyber-sex), work, gambling, oniomania (compulsive shopping).

> And take heed to yourselves, lest at any time your hearts be overcharged with surfeiting, and drunkenness, and cares of this life, and so that day come upon you unawares.
>
> —Luke 21:34

> Know ye not, that to whom ye yield yourselves servants to obey, his servants ye are to whom ye obey; whether of sin unto death, or of obedience unto righteousness?
>
> —Romans 6:16

Counterattack: Decree and declare that according to 1 Corinthians 6:19, _____ (insert name)'s body is the temple of the Holy Spirit. Break the stronghold of addiction. Ask God to remove the appetite for the thing or person. Establish God as the gatekeeper and doorkeeper of your soul. Ask God to bring healing and reconciliation to every person negatively affected by your addiction. Renounce future activities with anything or anyone associated with addictive activities. Ask God to eclipse the addiction with purpose. War in the spirit and decree and declare that all diabolical strongholds are destroyed, spirits of inheritances are severed and prohibited from influencing any future activities.

Adultery

Adultery is a voluntary sexual relationship between a married person and a person other than their spouse. It is a form of betrayal that involves the breaking of a covenant and is an elaborately crafted weapon of mass destruction. This satanic tool is used to corrode the institutions of marriage and family and ultimately causes the very fabric of a just and moral society or nation to fray at its seams. The adulterer or adulteress betrays their marriage vow, and lies in order to cover up their sin. The deceptive nature of adultery is that the individuals involved believe no one else is hurt by their activities. The feelings of betrayal, hurt, sadness, anger, and grief are caused not just because one of the partners engages in a sexual relationship with another, but also that the exclusivity and secrecy of the relationship causes feelings of betrayal and intense emotional pain. To know that your partner is sharing an intimate spiritual or emotional connection with someone else can be extremely disconcerting.

> He saith unto him, Which? Jesus said, Thou shalt do no murder, Thou shalt not commit adultery, Thou shalt not steal, Thou shalt not bear false witness.
> —MATTHEW 19:18

Counterattack: The first step toward resolution and healing is naming it for what it is, acknowledging that it happened rather than pretending it did not in the hope that it and the feelings associated with it would just go away. The act of adultery needs to be admitted rather than rationalized or defended. Next, the feelings need to be expressed, not explained, by both parties. There may be fear, anger, hurt, sadness, and grief, or even rage. Petition the Lord to help you to forgive and to empower you to move on in love. Break and renounce sexual soul ties. Ask for forgiveness. Ask God to restore commitment to covenant. Build a hedge of protection around your mind and body. Fast until the desire for the other individual is broken. Ask God to purify the mind by the blood, the Word, and the Spirit.

Adversity

Adversities are calamitous circumstances and conditions that cause anguish, affliction, distress, physical discomfort, and psychological damage. These life-altering and sometimes life-threatening events can be national, financial, physical, organizational, ministerial, spiritual, or psychological, in nature.

If thou faint in the day of adversity, thy strength is small.

—PROVERBS 24:10

Who now rejoice in my sufferings for you, and fill up that which is behind of the afflictions of Christ in my flesh for his body's sake, which is the church.

—COLOSSIANS 1:24

Counterattack: Quote Isaiah 59:19, "When the enemy shall come in like a flood, the Spirit of the LORD shall lift up a standard against him." Ask God to give you a strong support system to encourage and gird you up during times of adversity according to Proverbs 17:17.

Afflictions

An affliction is a pathological (deviation from normalcy) condition of mind, body, soul, or spirit that produces suffering, sicknesses, disease, or conditions difficult to treat, cure, or overcome by human interventions. The ultimate cure of course is divine intervention. The list of afflictions include:

- Trials/tribulations
- Sorrows of the soul (depression, rejection, inferiority complex, loneliness)
- Physical ailments
- Emotional hardship
- Misfortunes
- Satanically induced vexation
- Satanic/demonic provocation
- Incurable disease and sickness

- Adversity
- Abandonment
- Calamities and catastrophes
- Distress
- Medical emergencies

Counterattack: Quote Psalm 34:19, "Many are the afflictions of the righteous: but the Lord delivereth him out of them all." Ask God for divine intervention. Declare and decree that you are protected by *Jehovah Gibbor*, *Jehovah Nissi*, and *Jehovah Rapha*. Continue to build prayer shields, firewalls, and prayer hedges around yourself, loved ones, ministry, and business. Pray the prayers from volume 1 of *The Rules of Engagement*.

Anger

The Hebrew word for anger is *anaph* which when literally translated means, "rapid breathing from passion."[1] An angry person is often spoken of as someone who boils with anger, or who is hotheaded. This is because extreme anger affects every part of our being. The Holy Spirit's presence in our lives should be the gatekeeper to our soul. The enemy wants to make you or people associated with you emotional volcanoes, erratically erupting and disrupting peace. Don't let your (or anyone else's) hot temper and emotions get the best of you, creating irrational, ungodly responses and behavior, fear, trepidation, and hostile environments for others to live in. The enemy would love to have you live a life driven by anger rather than being led by the Spirit of God. He wants to make you an emotional puppet on a diabolical string and open prey to the enemy. According to Proverbs 25:28, "He that hath no rule over his own spirit is like a city that is broken down, and without walls."

> O my soul, come not thou into their secret; unto their assembly, mine honour, be not thou united: for in their anger they slew a man, and in their selfwill they digged down a wall. Cursed be their anger, for it was fierce; and their wrath, for it was cruel: I will divide them in Jacob, and scatter them in Israel.
>
> —Genesis 49:6–7

Counterattack: Decree and declare: "I will not be driven by anger but by the Holy Spirit." Ask God to release the fruit of the Spirit and let it saturate your soul. Bind every spirit that attempts to control your emotions. Claim John 8:36 for yourself and for anyone bound by the spirit of anger, "If the Son therefore shall make you free, ye shall be free indeed."

Anxiety

Anxiety is the apprehensive, uneasy, and distressed state of mind concerning real or imagined future possibilities, probabilities, or eventualities. This condition causes a kind of mental prison, which when not counteracted by faith in God, will invite fear, hopelessness, depression, worry, and dread to become fellow inmates who in turn will place your present and future on lockdown. To render this weapon ineffective, the apostle Paul encourages us to use our anxieties as prayer points and prophetic praise reports:

Be careful [anxious] for nothing; but in every thing by prayer and supplication with thanksgiving let your requests be made known unto God.

—Philippians 4:6

Counterattack: Pray Psalm 20:7, "Some trust in chariots, and some in horses: but we will remember the name of the Lord our God."

Apathy

When the spirit of apathy is present it causes a person to become indifferent and desensitized to circumstances or conditions, ultimately producing a literal numbing of the soul and an emotional calcification of the heart. Having spent many years in bondage, Satan attacked the children of Israel with this weapon. The psalmist recorded their blues in Psalm 137:1–4 (NIV), which states:

By the rivers of Babylon we sat and wept when we remembered Zion. There on the poplars we hung our harps, for there our captors asked us for songs, our tormentors demanded songs of joy; they said, "Sing us one of the songs of Zion!" How can we sing the songs of the Lord while in a foreign land?

Counterattack: Psalm 42:11, "Why art thou cast down, O my soul? and why art thou disquieted within me? hope thou in God: for I shall yet praise him, who is the health of my countenance, and my God." Bind the spirit of apathy and decree and declare that the anointing destroys every yoke and lifts every burden. Receive the joy of the Lord as your strength.

Approval-Seeking Activities

People who engage in approval-seeking activities are people who will do anything to get affirmation and acceptance from others. Approval seeking individuals lack personal power, self-worth/dignity, and significance. Approval seeking activities are fear-driven. The instigating spirit will cause you to fear negative responses and feedback, and to become so approval-dependent that you barter away all your time, energy, and personal preferences just for affirmation and approval. Sometimes these activities will come across as noble and altruistic. If you carefully examine the motivations behind most activities, you will notice they are usually instigated by the need to be seen, affirmed, or accepted. Activities can range from saying yes, when you really want or should say no (becoming a yes-man), or a total denial of self. But in saying no, deep down inside if you really explore what is going on, you are engaging in activities that invalidate your significance and importance as an individual free to make decisions independent of another's opinion.

Approval-seeking shenanigans will cause you to become a feel-good junky addicted to the affirmation of others and focusing solely on their affirmations. You let others have their way with you, say whatever they want to you, treat you any way they want, walk over you; treating you like a doormat in exchange for a hit of praise. Of course, you love when they call you good, godly, saintly, angelic. Your personal preference and opinion, critical thinking, purpose, vision, and desires are inconsequential when juxtaposed to another. You have been conditioned to believe that bad feelings or disappointments are not "normal" emotions and that you should always feel good and make others feel good, too. To say it another way, you have been seduced into believing that life should always feel good and people should always approve your activities, thoughts, and behaviors. This spirit will lead you to believe that if people disapprove of your actions, thoughts, or behaviors, or project their feelings and thoughts onto you, that this equals a disapproval of you as a person. People in your life are likely to reinforce your pathological condition because you will do anything to please others at your own expense. So, what's not to love about you?

Pleasing others can be richly rewarding especially when you do it because you really want to and it is an expression of compassion, love, and positive regard. It is an amazing, life-affirming way to strengthen a relationship, propel the vision of ministry, and undergird the efforts of others. However, when it is motivated by obligation, powerlessness, or calculated advantage it becomes the quintessential definition of degradation, self-betrayal, and self-abuse, destroying authenticity and integrity of self.

Counterattack: Ask God to restore your authentic self. Ask God to remove from your mental and psychological portfolio all attention-seeking activities and to place your feet on a path that leads you to a purpose-driven, principle-orientated life. Bind all feelings of powerlessness and ask God to restore your personal parameters of power, self-worth, and dignity. Loose the spirit which perpetuates irrational thought processes and make it a part of the footstool of Jesus according to Hebrews 1:13. Decree and declare that your affirmation comes from Psalm 139:14, and repeat, "I will praise thee; for I am fearfully and wonderfully made: marvellous are thy works; and that my soul knoweth right well."

Arguments

Arguments are carnal, self-centered, or demonically instigated verbal conflict, disagreement, or irrational presupposition presented to support an erroneous thought, opinion, or position. This weapon is used to seduce people away from the truth, to avoid responsibility, or is used as an alibi to cover the truth. Many relationships, ministries, and marriages end up sabotaged, undermined, or destroyed because of this particular weapon. At all costs, a child of God should avoid this kind of controversy because according to Titus 3:9 it is useless and unprofitable.

> Don't have anything to do with foolish and stupid arguments, because you know they produce quarrels.
> —2 TIMOTHY 2:23, NIV

Counterattack: Pray Titus 3:9, "But avoid foolish controversies and genealogies and arguments and quarrels about the law, because these are unprofitable and useless" (NIV).

Attachments

As the word suggests, an attachment is that which Satan uses to maintain alliances and connection to something that is not good for you or has the power to undermine and destroy purpose, potential, and destiny because it facilitates carnality and unrighteousness. An attachment can exist on many levels and take on many different forms such as food, people, conditions, environments, or behaviors. They can exist prior to salvation and long after a person receives the Lord as their Savior. A good example of this is contained in the account of Simon the Sorcerer in the Book of Acts. Even after his conversion, residue from his activities in the occult was still evident. Although he had been converted, he still needed deliverance:

> When Simon saw that the Spirit was given at the laying on of the apostles' hands, he offered them money and said, "Give me also this ability so that everyone on whom I lay my hands may receive the Holy Spirit." Peter answered: "May your money perish with you, because you thought you could buy the gift of God with money! You have no part or share in this ministry, because your heart is not right before God. Repent of this wickedness and pray to the Lord. Perhaps he will forgive you for having such a thought in your heart. For I see that you are full of bitterness and captive to sin." Then Simon answered, "Pray to the Lord for me so that nothing you have said may happen to me."
>
> —ACTS 8:18–24, NIV

Counterattack: Break all demonic and satanic attachments. Sever them by the blood and by the Spirit. Decree and declare that you are free from all alliance covenants and contracts that have not originated from the heart and mind of God.

Attention-Seeking Activities

In life you will run across people who will do anything to gain center stage and to be at the center of everyone's attention. These individuals usually are starved for attention, plagued with the spirit of jealousy, or just plain insecure.

Stemming from their upbringing this state usually is the result of having not received appropriate attention in their unique love language.

Counterattack: Pray Jeremiah 31:3, "The LORD hath appeared of old unto me, saying, Yea, I have loved thee with an everlasting love: therefore with lovingkindness have I drawn thee."

Avoidance

Avoidance activities are socially, emotionally, or psychologically generated disorders whereby a person shuns responsibilities, circumvents accountability through justification, excuses, or alibis. Usually a person who is skilled in this area will be seduced into living a hermit-type life, avoiding confrontational situations, uncomfortable conditions, or anything that moves them out of their abnormal comfort zone.

Counterattack: Decree and declare that according to 2 Timothy 1:7 and Psalm 18:29, "God hath not given us the spirit of fear; but of power, and of love, and of a sound mind," and "by thee I have run through a troop; and by my God have I leaped over a wall." Break the spirit of fear and irresponsibility.

Backlash

Backlash is the spiritual repercussion an individual experiences after making spiritual inroads in prayer and gaining new territories through spiritual warfare activities. This is satanic quid pro quo; like the saying goes: "You kill my cat, I'll kill your dog." Do not be intimidated. Be like David—don't give up or give in. Don't throw in the towel or raise a white flag of defeat. If the enemy causes any losses or setbacks, pursue, prevail, and recover all!

> And it came to pass, when David and his men were come to Ziklag on the third day, that the Amalekites had invaded the south, and Ziklag, and smitten Ziklag, and burned it with fire; and had taken the women captives, that were therein: they slew not any, either great or small, but carried them away, and went on their way. So David and his men came to the city, and, behold, it was burned with fire; and their wives, and their sons, and their daughters, were taken captives. Then David and the people that were with him lifted up their voice and wept, until they had no more power to weep. And David's two wives were taken captives, Ahinoam the Jezreelitess, and Abigail the wife of Nabal the Carmelite. And David was greatly distressed; for the people spake of stoning him, because the soul of all the people was grieved, every man for his sons and for his daughters: but David encouraged himself in the LORD his God. And David said to Abiathar the priest, Ahimelech's son, I pray thee, bring me hither the ephod. And Abiathar brought thither the ephod to David. And David inquired at the LORD, saying, Shall I pursue after this troop? shall I overtake them? And he answered him, Pursue: for thou shalt surely overtake them, and without fail recover all.
>
> —1 SAMUEL 30:1–8

Counterattack: Seek God for a divine strategy to counter the attack of the enemy. Gird up the loins of the mind with resolve that you cannot be overcome and defeated because, according to 1 John 4:4, "Greater is he that is in you, than he that is in the world."

Backsliding

The word *backsliding* is an old English term used to describe the regressive action of an individual who, having made progress toward a more ethically, morally, and spiritually-enriched life, reverts back to a less than admirable life of immorality, spiritual depravity, and spiritual and emotional immaturity. When the spirit of backsliding hits you, it has the potential to cause you to move out of a higher level of operating in the spirit to a lower, inferior state of existence.

The LORD said also unto me in the days of Josiah the king, Hast thou seen that which backsliding Israel hath done? she is gone up upon every high mountain and under every green tree, and there hath played the harlot. And I said after she had done all these things, Turn thou unto me. But she returned not. And her treacherous sister Judah saw it. And I saw, when for all the causes whereby backsliding Israel committed adultery I had put her away, and given her a bill of divorce; yet her treacherous sister Judah feared not, but went and played the harlot also. And it came to pass through the lightness of her whoredom, that she defiled the land, and committed adultery with stones and with stocks. And yet for all this her treacherous sister Judah hath not turned unto me with her whole heart, but feignedly, saith the LORD. And the LORD said unto me, The backsliding Israel hath justified herself more than treacherous Judah. Go and proclaim these words toward the north, and say, Return, thou backsliding Israel, saith the LORD; and I will not cause mine anger to fall upon you: for I am merciful, saith the LORD, and I will not keep anger for ever. Only acknowledge thine iniquity, that thou hast transgressed against the LORD thy God, and hast scattered thy ways to the strangers under every green tree, and ye have not obeyed my voice, saith the LORD. Turn, O backsliding children, saith the LORD; for I am married unto you: and I will take you one of a city, and two of a family, and I will bring you to Zion.

—JEREMIAH 3:6–14

Now we beseech you, brethren, by the coming of our Lord Jesus Christ, and by our gathering together unto him, that ye be not soon shaken in mind, or be troubled, neither by spirit, nor by word, nor by letter as from us, as that the day of Christ is at hand. Let no man deceive you by any means: for that day shall not come, except there come a falling away first, and that man of sin be revealed, the son of perdition.

—2 THESSALONIANS 2:1–3

Counterattack: Decree and declare that according to Hebrews 6:18–19, "[I] have a strong consolation…lay hold upon the hope set before us [me]: which hope we [I] have as an anchor of the [my] soul, both sure and stedfast," in Jesus' name. Ask God to make your feet like hind feet and to grant you spiritual stability.

Bad Reputations

In Philemon 1:10–11, Paul makes an appeal on behalf of a brother who apparently had a bad reputation. A reputation is the value, assessment, or a kind of social rating placed upon a person based on the perception of their character, image, and activities. The Bible clearly states that "man looketh on the outward appearance" (1 Sam. 16:7). We can have good reputations or bad reputations. Another person's assessment of us can be accurate or inaccurate. Perception is reality to the person perceiving. The enemy uses this fact to twist and distort our perceptions. If the enemy has used this, causing your reputation to be marred, pray for divine intervention. God can erase a bad reputation divinely, or use a person to facilitate the eradication.

Paul takes a similar stand in the Book of Colossians, intervening in the life of a young minister by the name of Onesimus. Paul was an excellent candidate to be divinely used by God because throughout his career, this was one of the many weapons the enemy employed against him in an attempt to destroy his influence and credibility as a man of integrity and authentic apostolic anointing. (See Acts 9:19–30.) If Satan is using this weapon against you, petition God to give you a good name in place of a bad one.

> With Onesimus, a faithful and beloved brother, who is one of you. They shall make known unto you all things which are done here.
>
> —COLOSSIANS 4:9

> I beseech thee for my son Onesimus, whom I have begotten in my bonds: which in time past was to thee

unprofitable, but now profitable to thee and to me.

—PHILEMON 1:10–11

Counterattack: Pray this prayer or a prayer similar to this: "Father, I cry out unto the God of Abraham, Isaac, and Jacob, the God who is able to change both my name and nature. According to Proverbs 22:1 and Ecclesiastes 7:1, You said in Your Word that a good name is better than precious ointments, and rather to be chosen than great riches. Therefore I decree and declare that my name is associated with holiness, righteousness, integrity, favor, and excellence. Give me a good name, amen."

Bands

In the Bible days, a band was a thin strip of flexible material used for encircling and the binding of one object to another, or to hold a number of objects together. Using this analogy, bands can therefore be referred to as satanic restraining devices that prohibit progress, growth, and development by causing a person to be bound to situations, circumstances, conditions, people, habits, thought and behavior patterns, activities, and substances. Bands can be physical, psychological, or emotional.

> I am the Lord your God, which brought you forth out of the land of Egypt, that ye should not be their bondmen; and I have broken the bands of your yoke, and made you go upright.

—LEVITICUS 26:13

Shake thyself from the dust; arise, and sit down, O Jerusalem: loose thyself from the bands of thy neck, O captive daughter of Zion.

—Isaiah 52:2

Is not this the fast that I have chosen? to loose the bands of wickedness, to undo the heavy burdens, and to let the oppressed go free, and that ye break every yoke?

—Isaiah 58:6

Counterattack: Pray: "Father, please free me from the bands of wickedness." Utilize the power of the weapons of "prayer and fasting." (See Matthew 17:21.)

Besetting Sin

According to the following text, a besetting sin would be any hindrance that Satan uses to thwart the progress of a believer so that he cannot finish a particular course of action.

Wherefore seeing we also are compassed about with so great a cloud of witnesses, let us lay aside every weight, and the sin which doth so easily beset us, and let us run with patience the race that is set before us.

—Hebrews 12:1

Counterattack: Pray according to Psalm 51:1–19:

Have mercy upon me, O God, according to thy lovingkindness: according unto the multitude of thy tender mercies blot out my transgressions. Wash me throughly from mine iniquity, and cleanse me from my sin. For I acknowledge my transgressions: and my

43

sin is ever before me. Against thee, thee only, have I sinned, and done this evil in thy sight: that thou mightest be justified when thou speakest, and be clear when thou judgest. Behold, I was shapen in iniquity; and in sin did my mother conceive me. Behold, thou desirest truth in the inward parts: and in the hidden part thou shalt make me to know wisdom. Purge me with hyssop, and I shall be clean: wash me, and I shall be whiter than snow. Make me to hear joy and gladness; that the bones which thou hast broken may rejoice. Hide thy face from my sins, and blot out all mine iniquities. Create in me a clean heart, O God; and renew a right spirit within me. Cast me not away from thy presence; and take not thy holy spirit from me. Restore unto me the joy of thy salvation; and uphold me with thy free spirit. Then will I teach transgressors thy ways; and sinners shall be converted unto thee. Deliver me from bloodguiltiness, O God, thou God of my salvation: and my tongue shall sing aloud of thy righteousness. O Lord, open thou my lips; and my mouth shall shew forth thy praise. For thou desirest not sacrifice; else would I give it: thou delightest not in burnt offering. The sacrifices of God are a broken spirit: a broken and a contrite heart, O God, thou wilt not despise. Do good in thy good pleasure unto Zion: build thou the walls of Jerusalem. Then shalt thou be pleased with the sacrifices of righteousness, with burnt offering and whole burnt offering: then shall they offer bullocks upon thine altar.

Betrayal

Betrayal is a powerful weapon that robs a person of his or her trust in something or someone through the violation of covenant, contracts, or verbal agreements. This weapon causes intense grief of the soul. There are two pieces of advice I want to give you if you have been betrayed. First, never allow yourself to take on the role of a victim. And second, do not give your personal power away. Remember, you have a God who will never betray you. He has made a covenant with you that He will never break.

> My heart is sore pained within me: and the terrors of death are fallen upon me. Fearfulness and trembling are come upon me, and horror hath overwhelmed me. And I said, Oh that I had wings like a dove! for then would I fly away, and be at rest....For it was not an enemy that reproached me; then I could have borne it: neither was it he that hated me that did magnify himself against me; then I would have hid myself from him: but it was thou, a man mine equal, my guide, and mine acquaintance. We took sweet counsel together, and walked unto the house of God in company.
>
> —PSALM 55:4–6, 12–14

Counterattack: Pray this prayer: "Father, as You heal me of my heart of disappointment, bitterness, sadness, anger, rage, and pain, I thank You for all of Your promises. Help me to believe again and to trust again. Amen." (See 1 Corinthians 1:20.) Remember that your hope is in God.

Bitterness

Bitterness, the fruit of unforgiveness, causes deep-seated resentment, hatred, and ill will. This acrimonious emotion is the result of anguish, disappointment, or severe grief. It is believed by many psychotherapeutic practitioners and spiritual leaders that bitterness is the root cause of arthritis and a host of other emotional, spiritual, psychological, and physiological maladies. Bitterness is a weapon that once effectively utilized against you will affect every facet of your life. It erodes relationships, taints the perception, contaminates the anointing, and hinders true liberty in the spirit. The spirit of bitterness, acting as a doorkeeper, will make its victim hostile, antagonistic, acrimonious, and open to other demonic activities.

> Thy way and thy doings have procured these things unto thee; this is thy wickedness, because it is bitter, because it reacheth unto thine heart.
>
> —JEREMIAH 4:18

> Looking diligently lest any man fail of the grace of God; lest any root of bitterness springing up trouble you, and thereby many be defiled.
>
> —HEBREWS 12:15

Counterattack: Choose to let go and forgive. Ask God to remove the root of bitterness from you and to allow His grace to permeate your mind, soul, and emotions.

Blind Spots

Have you ever had anyone point out a proclivity, action, habit, or attitude that you supposedly had demonstrated and that you swore was incorrect? Do you know anyone that no matter how many people accuse them of saying or doing something they simply cannot see what people are referring to? Have you ever been told something about yourself by more than one person which you flatly deny because you cannot see what they are talking about? This is what we call a blind spot. They are things in our lives that we do that offend, hurt, or insult others that we are unaware of. Remember, even if a person points these things out to you, and are obvious to others, you will not be able to see what they are talking about or referring to.

> Behold, thou desirest truth in the inward parts: and in the hidden part thou shalt make me to know wisdom.
>
> —PSALM 51:6

> But their minds were blinded: for until this day remaineth the same vail untaken away in the reading of the old testament; which vail is done away in Christ.
>
> —2 CORINTHIANS 3:14

> In whom the god of this world hath blinded the minds of them which believe not, lest the light of the glorious gospel of Christ, who is the image of God, should shine unto them.
>
> —2 CORINTHIANS 4:4

Counterattack: Ask God to reveal to you the truth about yourself and to deliver you from any attitude, behavior, or action that hinders healthy interactions with others. Ask God to remove all spiritual blindness and veils so that you truly can live a life of personal integrity and authenticity of self in Jesus' name.

Bondages

Bondage is a condition wherein a person is placed in a state of subjugation to an "owner" or a "master" who psychologically, emotionally, or physically restrains them by force, power, or influence. Bondage has many faces, wears many masks, and creates emotional, physical, financial, and spiritual prisoners out of its victims. People can be in bondage to such things as drugs, alcohol, and sex.

> And Moses said unto the people, Remember this day, in which ye came out from Egypt, out of the house of bondage; for by strength of hand the LORD brought you out from this place: there shall no leavened bread be eaten.
>
> —EXODUS 13:3

Counterattack: "The Spirit of the LORD GOD is upon me; because the LORD hath anointed me to preach good tidings unto the meek; he hath sent me to bind up the brokenhearted, to proclaim liberty to the captives, and the opening of the prison to them that are bound; to proclaim the acceptable year of the LORD, and the day of vengeance of our God; to comfort all that mourn; to appoint unto them that mourn in Zion, to give unto them beauty for ashes, the oil of joy for mourning, the garment of praise for the spirit of heaviness; that they might be called trees of righteousness, the planting of the LORD, that he might be glorified" (Isa. 61:1–3).

Cares of This World

Cares of the world can be anything causing a believer to pursue worldly things, business ventures, and the acquisition of possessions at the expense of their pursuit of God, His Word, and His Kingdom.

> He also that received seed among the thorns is he that heareth the word; and the care of this world, and the deceitfulness of riches, choke the word, and he becometh unfruitful.
>
> —MATTHEW 13:22

Counterattack: Read Colossians 2:20–21, "Wherefore if ye be dead with Christ from the rudiments of the world, why, as though living in the world, are ye subject to ordinances, (Touch not; taste not; handle not)." Then read Matthew 6:33, "But seek ye first the kingdom of God, and his righteousness; and all these things shall be added unto you."

Carnality

Carnality is the appetite of the flesh and soul. It is the preoccupation with one's appetite and satiation of urges, drives, and desires. (See *The Rules of Engagement, Vol. 2: Binding the Strongman,* for more information and an in-depth study of this spirit.)

For ye are yet carnal: for whereas there is among you envying, and strife, and divisions, are ye not carnal, and walk as men? For while one saith, I am of Paul; and another, I am of Apollos; are ye not carnal?

—1 CORINTHIANS 3:3–4

Counterattack: "This I say then, Walk in the Spirit, and ye shall not fulfil the lust of the flesh" (Gal. 5:16).

Celestial Barricades

Have you ever prayed and it felt like your prayers were just hitting the ceiling? Have you ever attempted to pursue a God-given idea, mandate, or mission only to feel as if every attempt was hindered by some unseen force? You might have encountered what I call a "celestial barricade." Celestial barricades are satanic maneuvers, barriers, blocks, encumbrances, and hindrances that obstruct, hinder, and prohibit movement in the spirit realm and frustrate the progress of a vision, dream, mandate, mission, prayer, or the plan of God for your life.

Then said he unto me, Fear not, Daniel: for from the first day that thou didst set thine heart to understand, and to chasten thyself before thy God, thy words were heard, and I am come for thy words. But the prince of the kingdom of Persia withstood me one and twenty days: but, lo, Michael, one of the chief princes, came to help me; and I remained there with the kings of Persia.

—DANIEL 10:12–13

Counterattack: Use a combination of prayer and fasting. Reinforce your prayer efforts by engaging in the prayer of agreement. Ask God to send divine angelic assistance to remove all hindrances and barriers in Jesus' name.

Chains/Fetters/Shackles

Chains, fetters, and shackles are anything that confine movement, hinder progress, and cause captivity, oppression, and bondage.

> God setteth the solitary in families: he bringeth out those which are bound with chains: but the rebellious dwell in a dry land.
>
> —Psalm 68:6

And the lords of the Philistines came up unto her, and said unto her, Entice him, and see wherein his great strength lieth, and by what means we may prevail against him, that we may bind him to afflict him: and we will give thee every one of us eleven hundred pieces of silver. And Delilah said to Samson, Tell me, I pray thee, wherein thy great strength lieth, and wherewith thou mightest be bound to afflict thee....And when Delilah saw that he had told her all his heart, she sent and called for the lords of the Philistines, saying, Come up this once, for he hath shewed me all his heart. Then the lords of the Philistines came up unto her, and brought money in their hand. And she made him sleep upon her knees; and she called for a man, and she caused him to shave off the seven locks of his head; and she began to afflict him, and his strength went from him. And she said, The Philistines be upon thee, Samson. And he awoke out of his sleep, and said, I will go out as at other times before, and shake myself. And he wist not that the LORD was departed from him. But the Philistines took him, and put out his eyes, and brought him down to Gaza, and bound him with fetters of brass; and he did grind in the prison house.

—JUDGES 16:5–6, 18–21

Counterattack: "Let the high praises of God be in their mouth, and a twoedged sword in their hand; to execute vengeance upon the heathen, and punishments upon the people; to bind their kings with chains, and their nobles with fetters of iron; to execute upon them the judgment written: this honour have all his saints. Praise ye the LORD" (Ps. 149:6–9).

Complacency

Adam and Eve were prosperous until complacency set in. Israel had begun to become socially and politically prosperous under the leadership of Joshua until the spirit of complacency set in. Complacency kills passion, strangles drive and motivation, and lulls a person's senses to sleep until they are unaware of their deficiencies, their need for God, and the need to do something about their condition. This spirit is so powerful that it will cause you to lose your sense of urgency, vigilance, and awareness, and to walk through life unconscious.

Awake to righteousness, and sin not; for some have not the knowledge of God: I speak this to your shame.
—1 CORINTHIANS 15:34

Wherefore he saith, Awake thou that sleepest, and arise from the dead, and Christ shall give thee light.
—EPHESIANS 5:14

Counterattack: Ask God to grant you an alertness of mind, zeal, and an urgency of spirit. Pray the following verses, "See then that ye walk circumspectly, not as fools, but as wise, redeeming the time, because the days are evil. Wherefore be ye not unwise, but understanding what the will of the Lord is" (Eph. 5:15–17).

Compromising

The enemy uses this weapon to cause you to make concessions to things that are spiritually detrimental. In the case of a believer, it is the lowering of a biblical standard and the abatement of a conviction.

Let not then your good be evil spoken of.
—ROMANS 14:16

A double minded man is unstable in all his ways.
—JAMES 1:8

Counterattack: Bind the compromising spirit. Superimpose the spirits of conviction, excellence, and resolve.

Condemnation

The spirit of condemnation causes mental and emotional torment by satanically imposing an overwhelming sense of guilt, long-term remorse, and shame in spite of a confessed sin and a repented heart. Remember—God convicts, Satan condemns.

> There is therefore now no condemnation to them which are in Christ Jesus, who walk not after the flesh, but after the Spirit.
>
> —ROMANS 8:1

Counterattack: "If the Son therefore shall make you free, ye shall be free indeed" (John 8:36). "For God sent not his Son into the world to condemn the world; but that the world through him might be saved" (John 3:17).

Confederates

A confederate is one who supports another in a criminal act as an accomplice or an ally. (See *The Rules of Engagement, Vol. 2: Binding the Strongman* for an in-depth study of this spirit.)

> For they have consulted together with one consent: they are confederate against thee.
>
> —PSALM 83:5

> And it was told the house of David, saying, Syria is confederate with Ephraim. And his heart was moved, and the heart of his people, as the trees of the wood are moved with the wind.
>
> —ISAIAH 7:2

Counterattack: Decree and declare that God will confuse the communications of every satanically orchestrated confederation and disperse their gatherings. Pray *The Rules of Engagement, Vol. 1: The Art of Strategic Prayer and Spiritual Warfare.*

Contaminated Anointing

A contaminated anointing is caused when someone who is ministering ministers without full and total submission to the Holy Spirit. The pure anointing becomes contaminated because it flows from the soulish realm rather than a regenerated and consecrated spirit.

> But these speak evil of those things which they know not: but what they know naturally, as brute beasts, in those things they corrupt themselves. Woe unto them! for they have gone in the way of Cain, and ran greedily after the error of Balaam for reward, and perished in the gainsaying of Core. These are spots in your feasts of charity, when they feast with you, feeding themselves without fear: clouds they are without water, carried about of winds; trees whose fruit withereth, without fruit, twice dead, plucked up by the roots; raging waves of the sea, foaming out their own shame; wandering stars, to whom is reserved the blackness of darkness for ever.
>
> —JUDE 1:10–13

Counterattack: Decree and declare a fresh supply of the uncontaminated anointing begins to flow. Ask God to sanctify your soul and spirit according to Titus 3:5

by the washing of regeneration and renewing of the Holy Ghost.

Covert Operations

Covert operations are high-powered, camouflaged, satanic strategies used to hinder and frustrate the work of the Lord, to distract ministers, to destroy their influence and ministry, and to utterly destroy the lives of saints in general.

And a certain woman named Lydia, a seller of purple, of the city of Thyatira, which worshipped God, heard us: whose heart the Lord opened, that she attended unto the things which were spoken of Paul. And when she was baptized, and her household, she besought us, saying, If ye have judged me to be faithful to the Lord, come into my house, and abide there. And she constrained us. And it came to pass, as we went to prayer, a certain damsel possessed with a spirit of divination met us, which brought her masters much gain by soothsaying: the same followed Paul and us, and cried, saying, These men are the servants of the most high God, which shew unto us the way of salvation. And this did she many days. But Paul, being grieved, turned and said to the spirit, I command thee in the name of Jesus Christ to come out of her. And he came out the same hour. And when her masters saw that the hope of their gains was gone, they caught Paul and Silas, and drew them into the marketplace unto the rulers, and brought them to the magistrates, saying, These men, being Jews, do exceedingly trouble our city.

—ACTS 16:14–20

Counterattack: Ask God to expose, destroy, and dismantle every diabolical covert operation. Let the destroying winds of the Spirit blow in judgment against every work of darkness in Jesus' name. Declare and decree Isaiah 54:17, "No weapon that is formed against thee shall prosper; and every tongue that shall rise against thee in judgment thou shalt condemn. This is the heritage of the servants of the LORD, and their righteousness is of me, saith the Lord."

Covetousness

Covetousness causes an individual to lust for what rightfully belongs to others. This spirit acts as a doorkeeper to jealousy, hatred, envy, strife, murder, slander, adultery, and a host of other evil works of the flesh.

> For this, Thou shalt not commit adultery, Thou shalt not kill, Thou shalt not steal, Thou shalt not bear false witness, Thou shalt not covet; and if there be any other commandment, it is briefly comprehended in this saying, namely, Thou shalt love thy neighbour as thyself.
> —ROMANS 13:9

Counterattack: Pray the following verses, "The meek shall eat and be satisfied: they shall praise the LORD that seek him: your heart shall live for ever" (Ps. 22:26); "Not that I speak in respect of want: for I have learned, in whatsoever state I am, therewith to be content" (Phil. 4:11).

Culture

Cultures form when two or more individuals band together in response to perceived needs and then combine their abilities and resources to meet those needs. Once formed, cultures are responsible for socially transmitting behavior patterns, arts, beliefs, institutions, and all other products of human work and thought. Culture shapes your awareness of everything around you and how you react to things. Many times the enemy attempts to seduce believers into placing more emphasis on their earthly culture rather than the culture of the kingdom of God, which takes precedence over all national, organizational, and parochial cultures.

Then Philip went down to the city of Samaria, and preached Christ unto them. And the people with one accord gave heed unto those things which Philip spake, hearing and seeing the miracles which he did. For unclean spirits, crying with loud voice, came out of many that were possessed with them: and many taken with palsies, and that were lame, were healed. And there was great joy in that city. But there was a certain man, called Simon, which beforetime in the same city used sorcery, and bewitched the people of Samaria, giving out that himself was some great one: to whom they all gave heed, from the least to the greatest, saying, This man is the great power of God. And to him they had regard, because that of long time he had bewitched them with sorceries. But when they believed Philip preaching the things concerning the kingdom of God, and the name of Jesus Christ, they were baptized, both men and women. Then Simon himself believed also: and when he was baptized, he continued with Philip, and wondered, beholding the miracles and signs which were done.

—Acts 8:5–13

Counterattack: "And be not conformed to this world: but be ye transformed by the renewing of your mind, that ye may prove what is that good, and acceptable, and perfect, will of God. Superimpose the culture of the Kingdom of Heaven, over all opposing cultures" (Rom. 12:2). Decree and declare Luke 11:2, "Thy kingdom come. Thy will be done, as in heaven, so in earth."

Death

Death is the most deadly weapon Satan has in his arsenal (pun intended). It demands the attention of humanity and the curiosity of science. It commands the attention of all media and culture. It promotes the sale of newspapers, books, and life insurance and provides plots for Hollywood. Death even has a way of causing people to carefully weigh their actions from the perspective of eternity. Death incorporates those occurrences that are untimely and unexpected such as suicides, homicides, accidents, loss of reputation, loss of hope, or divorce. The pain and agony experienced by those mourning their losses are often so intense and unbearable that they become vulnerable to its seduction and swept away into eternity by its dark and spindly hands. Untimely death aborts destinies, executes purpose, and assassinates potential.

For death is come up into our windows, and is entered into our palaces, to cut off the children from without, and the young men from the streets.

—JEREMIAH 9:21

Counterattack: Declare Romans 8:2: "For the law of the Spirit of life in Christ Jesus hath made me free from the law of sin and death"; Psalm 118:17: "I shall not die, but live, and declare the works of the LORD"; and 1 Corinthians 15:55: "O death, where is thy sting? O grave, where is thy victory?"

Deception

This weapon causes fraudulence, duplicity, underhandedness, cheating, and the willful betrayal of confidence and trust. This surreptitious behavior requires you to be vigilant, alert, and discerning of the spirits working and lurking around you. Take nothing and no one for granted. Although the enemy uses all forms of deception, the highest form of deception is self-deception. Deuteronomy 11:16 warns us to "take heed to yourselves, that your heart be not deceived, and ye turn aside, and serve other gods, and worship them."

And it came to pass, when all the kings which were on this side Jordan, in the hills, and in the valleys, and in all the coasts of the great sea over against Lebanon, the Hittite, and the Amorite, the Canaanite, the Perizzite, the Hivite, and the Jebusite, heard thereof; that they gathered themselves together, to fight with Joshua and with Israel, with one accord. And when the inhabitants of Gibeon heard what Joshua had done unto Jericho and to Ai, they did work wilily, and went and made as if they had been ambassadors, and took old sacks upon their asses, and wine bottles, old, and rent, and bound up; and old shoes and clouted upon their feet, and old garments upon them; and all the bread of their provision was dry and mouldy. And they went to Joshua unto the camp at Gilgal, and said unto him, and to the men of Israel, We be come from a far country: now therefore make ye a league with us. And the men of Israel said unto the Hivites, Peradventure ye dwell among us; and how shall we make a league with you? And they said unto Joshua, We are thy servants. And Joshua said unto them, Who are ye? and from whence come ye? And they said unto him, From a very far country thy servants are come because of the name of the Lord thy God: for we have heard the fame of him, and all that he did in Egypt, and all that he did to the two kings of the Amorites, that were beyond Jordan, to Sihon king of Heshbon, and to Og king of Bashan, which was at Ashtaroth. Wherefore our elders and all the inhabitants of our country spake to us, saying, Take victuals with you for the journey, and go to meet them, and say unto them, We are your servants: therefore now make ye a league with us. This our bread we took hot for our provision out of our houses on the day we came forth to go unto you; but now, behold, it is dry, and it is mouldy.

—Joshua 9:1–12

Know ye not that the unrighteous shall not inherit the kingdom of God? Be not deceived: neither fornicators, nor idolaters, nor adulterers, nor effeminate, nor abusers of themselves with mankind.

—1 CORINTHIANS 6:9

But evil men and seducers shall wax worse and worse, deceiving, and being deceived.

—2 TIMOTHY 3:13

Counterattack: "Howbeit when he, the Spirit of truth, is come, he will guide you into all truth: for he shall not speak of himself; but whatsoever he shall hear, that shall he speak: and he will shew you things to come" (John 16:13). "We are of God: he that knoweth God heareth us; he that is not of God heareth not us. Hereby know we the spirit of truth, and the spirit of error" (1 John 4:6).

Degenerative Diseases

From the moment we are conceived, the processes of life are carried out by our biological executor called DNA. Our DNA holds the genetic code for our life, health, and for the unique physical features of our bodies. DNA has the divine blueprint for our body, programming our cells to maintain optimum health from birth to death. The body is a magnificent biological system which provides an earth-suit for our spirits and, once filled by the Holy Spirit, provides a vessel through which God conducts His affairs in the earth realm. Degenerative diseases are the means by which Satan interferes with the life God wants for us all.

After this there was a feast of the Jews; and Jesus went up to Jerusalem. Now there is at Jerusalem by the sheep market a pool, which is called in the Hebrew tongue Bethesda, having five porches. In these lay a great multitude of impotent folk, of blind, halt, withered, waiting for the moving of the water. For an angel went down at a certain season into the pool, and troubled the water: whosoever then first after the troubling of the water stepped in was made whole of whatsoever disease he had. And a certain man was there, which had an infirmity thirty and eight years. When Jesus saw him lie, and knew that he had been now a long time in that case, he saith unto him, Wilt thou be made whole?

—JOHN 5:1–6

His flesh is consumed away, that it cannot be seen; and his bones that were not seen stick out.

—JOB 33:21

I am poured out like water, and all my bones are out of joint: my heart is like wax; it is melted in the midst of my bowels. My strength is dried up like a potsherd; and my tongue cleaveth to my jaws; and thou hast brought me into the dust of death. For dogs have compassed me: the assembly of the wicked have inclosed me: they pierced my hands and my feet. I may tell all my bones: they look and stare upon me.

—PSALM 22:14–17

Counterattack: Decree and declare that by the precious blood of Jesus, all sickness, ailments, degenerative conditions, and disease are healed. I am liberated from generational, satanic, demonic, alliances, allegiances, curses, and spirits of inheritance. I sever them by the sword of the Lord. He is *Jehovah Ropha*, the Lord that heals me. I speak to my DNA and declare that I am free from any and all influences passed down from one generation to another, biologically, socially, emotionally, physiologically, psychologically, nutritionally, spiritually, or by any other channel unknown to me but known to God. Decree and declare total divine alignment genetically, systemically, psychologically, bio-chemically, physiologically, cranially, and neurologically. Ensure you are feeding your body nutritious fresh fruit and vegetables, drinking sufficient water, exercising, and laughing at least seven times a day. I arbitrarily selected the number seven because it is God's perfect number. "A merry heart doeth good like a medicine: but a broken spirit drieth the bones" (Prov. 17:22).

Delusion

This weapon causes man to hold on to false perceptions, images, concepts, beliefs, and opinions generated by demons, embracing them as if they were truth and reality. The delusion may manifest itself as any of the following types:

Persecutory: the individual believes he or she is being threatened or mistreated by others.

Grandiose: the individual believes that they are extraordinarily important people or are possessed of extraordinary power, knowledge, or ability.

Jealous: the individual focuses on the suspected unfaithfulness of a spouse or sexual partner.

"Erotimatic": an individual convinces themselves that some person of eminence (usually whom they do not have close contact with, or have never met but with whom they frequently have corresponded) is in love with them.

Somatic: a false belief focused on a delusional physical abnormality or disorder, like false pregnancies.

Folie à deux: an extremely rare type of shared delusion, resulting from a close relationship with someone else who already has a delusions disorder.

> And for this cause God shall send them strong delusion, that they should believe a lie.
>
> —2 Thessalonians 2:11

Counterattack: "And ye shall know the truth, and the truth shall make you free" (John 8:32). Bind every spirit that twists and perverts your mind and thoughts. Ask God to place truth in your heart and to deliver you from all delusions.

Depression

Depression has become a prevalent mental disease in our world today. This weapon causes psychotic or neurotic conditions, and emotional and physiological disorders. It is characterized by an inability to concentrate, insomnia, and constant feelings of extreme sadness, lack of motivation, irritability, withdrawal tendencies, weight loss or gain, loneliness, fatigue, and thoughts of suicide, especially when the spirit of hopelessness sets in. As the word implies, it creates an overall feeling of heaviness. This spirit attacked Elijah, David, and Jesus. While Jesus overcame his depression through prayer and David through the reading of God's Word, Elijah overcame his depression though divine intervention. God instructed him to get up and get going.

> Then saith he unto them, My soul is exceeding sorrowful, even unto death: tarry ye here, and watch with me.
> —MATTHEW 26:38

> Reproach hath broken my heart; and I am full of heaviness: and I looked for some to take pity, but there was none; and for comforters, but I found none.
> —PSALM 69:20

> My soul melteth for heaviness: strengthen thou me according unto thy word.
> —PSALM 119:28

Counterattack: "To appoint unto them that mourn in Zion, to give unto them beauty for ashes, the oil of joy for mourning, the garment of praise for the spirit of heaviness; that they might be called trees of righteousness, the planting of the LORD, that he might be glorified" (Isa. 61:3). Ask God to remove the spirit of heaviness. Get up, open your curtains, and help someone less fortunate than you (visit the hospital, read to someone in the nursing home), start journaling, sing, dance, read the Word of God, play soothing music, go outside, worship, fellowship. Rebuke the spirit of depression. Decree and declare—the joy of the Lord is my strength.

Deprivation

Deprivation is the condition of being extremely poor, destitute. It divests a person of his or her God-given dignity and a good quality of life. Deprivation falls under the following categories:

Social deprivation: being restrained from enjoying interaction with certain people based on social-economic differences.

Sleep deprivation: extended periods of wakefulness or a decrease in sleep over an extended period.

Privacy deprivation: the divestment of the right to be free of unsanctioned intrusion.

Parental deprivation: physical and emotional detachment of parent from children.

Financial deprivation: withdrawal of financial support; loss of income; unemployment; underemployment resulting in a lack of money for food, housing, clothing, and transportation.

Early childhood deprivation: insufficient or lack of food, housing, clothing, safety, nurturance, love, guidance, care, concern, or direction.

Emotional deprivation: privation of affection, attention, direction, empathy, nurturance, strength, and understanding.

And there was a great famine in Samaria: and, behold, they besieged it, until an ass's head was sold for fourscore pieces of silver, and the fourth part of a cab of dove's dung for five pieces of silver.

—2 KINGS 6:25

Counterattack: Bind the spirit of deprivation and decree and declare that through divine intervention rivers of success, progress, and prosperity begin to flow. Decree and declare that the anointing of Cyrus is released and it flows according to Isaiah 45:1–3, "Thus saith the LORD to his anointed, to Cyrus, whose right hand I have holden, to subdue nations before him; and I will loose the loins of kings, to open before him the two leaved gates; and the gates shall not be shut; I will go before thee, and make the crooked places straight: I will break in pieces the gates of brass, and cut in sunder the bars of iron: And I will give thee the treasures of darkness, and hidden riches of secret places, that thou mayest know that I, the LORD, which call thee by thy name, am the God of Israel.

Discouragement

Many believers suffer from feelings of hopelessness in their Christian walk and ministry. These emotions are characteristic of the spirit of discouragement that occurs when a particular expectation is unmet:

> Why art thou cast down, O my soul? and why art thou disquieted in me? hope thou in God: for I shall yet praise him for the help of his countenance.

—PSALM 42:5

Counterattack: Pray these Bible passages, "My soul, wait thou only upon God; for my expectation is from him" (Ps.

62:5); "The hope of the righteous shall be gladness: but the expectation of the wicked shall perish" (Prov. 10:28).

Disillusionment

Disillusionment is a powerful weapon of divination that causes a feeling of deep, sorrowful unhappiness and woe. This psychological weapon was forged and successfully used against Elijah, one of the most powerful prophets in the Bible. After experiencing a great victory over the infernal enemies of Israel, Satan retaliated with a death threat issued through the mouth of Jezebel. This affected Elijah so deeply that he was prepared to give up everything, including his life:

> And Ahab told Jezebel all that Elijah had done, and withal how he had slain all the prophets with the sword. Then Jezebel sent a messenger unto Elijah, saying, So let the gods do to me, and more also, if I make not thy life as the life of one of them by to morrow about this time. And when he saw that, he arose, and went for his life, and came to Beer-sheba, which belongeth to Judah, and left his servant there. But he himself went a day's journey into the wilderness, and came and sat down under a juniper tree: and he requested for himself that he might die; and said, It is enough; now, O LORD, take away my life; for I am not better than my fathers.
>
> —1 KINGS 19:1–4

Counterattack: Gird up your mind. Pray without ceasing. Bind the spirit of disillusionment. Ask God to give you a vision of a future characterized by success, and to bring your life back into divine alignment. "Put on the whole armour of God, that ye may be able to stand against the wiles of the devil" (Eph. 6:1l).

Disobedience

Disobedience is the disposition that defies and resists authority, and the refusal or failure to obey a mandate, directive, or command. It is rebellion against known authority. According to 1 Samuel 15:23, God considers disobedience a form of witchcraft. The thought of disobedience being associated with witchcraft is chilling to me, especially as it relates to believers who sincerely love the Lord and want to serve Him. First Peter 2:13–15 encourages you to "submit yourselves to every ordinance of man for the Lord's sake: whether it be to the king, as supreme; or unto governors, as unto them that are sent by him for the punishment of evildoers, and for the praise of them that do well. For so is the will of God, that with well doing ye may put to silence the ignorance of foolish men."

> Samuel also said unto Saul, The LORD sent me to anoint thee to be king over his people, over Israel: now therefore hearken thou unto the voice of the words of the LORD. Thus saith the LORD of hosts, I remember that which Amalek did to Israel, how he laid wait for him in the way, when he came up from Egypt. Now go and smite Amalek, and utterly destroy all that they have, and spare them not; but slay both man and woman, infant and suckling, ox and sheep, camel and ass...And Samuel came to Saul: and Saul said unto him, Blessed be thou of the LORD: I have

performed the commandment of the LORD. And Samuel said, What meaneth then this bleating of the sheep in mine ears, and the lowing of the oxen which I hear? And Saul said, They have brought them from the Amalekites: for the people spared the best of the sheep and of the oxen, to sacrifice unto the LORD thy God; and the rest we have utterly destroyed. Then Samuel said unto Saul, Stay, and I will tell thee what the LORD hath said to me this night. And he said unto him, Say on. And Samuel said, When thou wast little in thine own sight, wast thou not made the head of the tribes of Israel, and the LORD anointed thee king over Israel? And the LORD sent thee on a journey, and said, Go and utterly destroy the sinners the Amalekites, and fight against them until they be consumed. Wherefore then didst thou not obey the voice of the LORD, but didst fly upon the spoil, and didst evil in the sight of the LORD? And Saul said unto Samuel, Yea, I have obeyed the voice of the LORD, and have gone the way which the LORD sent me, and have brought Agag the king of Amalek, and have utterly destroyed the Amalekites. But the people took of the spoil, sheep and oxen, the chief of the things which should have been utterly destroyed, to sacrifice unto the LORD thy God in Gilgal. And Samuel said, Hath the LORD as great delight in burnt offerings and sacrifices, as in obeying the voice of the LORD? Behold, to obey is better than sacrifice, and to hearken than the fat of rams. For rebellion is as the sin of witchcraft, and stubbornness is as iniquity and idolatry. Because thou hast rejected the word of the LORD, he hath also rejected thee from being king. And Saul said unto Samuel, I have sinned: for I have transgressed the commandment of the LORD, and thy words: because I feared the people, and obeyed their voice.

—1 SAMUEL 15:1–3, 13–24

Counterattack: Pray these verses: "Submit yourselves to every ordinance of man for the Lord's sake: whether it be to the king, as supreme" (1 Pet. 2:13). "Likewise, ye younger, submit yourselves unto the elder. Yea, all of you be subject one to another, and be clothed with humility: for God resisteth the proud, and giveth grace to the humble" (1 Pet. 5:5). "In that I command thee this day to love the LORD thy God, to walk in his ways, and to keep his commandments and his statutes and his judgments, that thou mayest live and multiply: and the LORD thy God shall bless thee in the land whither thou goest to possess it" (Deut. 30:16).

Divination

Divination, a word used interchangeably with witchcraft, is characterized by occult activities, deception, control, and fear. Individuals utilize satanic and diabolical agents, tactics, and strategies for the purposes of foretelling events and controlling people, animals, environments, things, and situations. Their tactics involve:

- Ill-spoken words
- Ill wishes
- Enchantments
- Spells
- Hexes
- Curses
- Witchcraft prayers

- Idle words spoken contrary to God's original plans and purposes
- Talisman
- Astrology
- Palmistry
- Crystal gazing
- Fortune-telling
- False prophecy
- Soothsaying
- Doctrines of devils

For a more comprehensive look at the spirit of divination, please refer to *The Rules of Engagement, Vol. 2: Binding the Strongman*.

Therefore hearken not ye to your prophets, nor to your diviners, nor to your dreamers, nor to your enchanters, nor to your sorcerers, which speak unto you, saying, Ye shall not serve the king of Babylon.

—JEREMIAH 27:9

Thou shalt not suffer a witch to live.

—EXODUS 22:18

There shall not be found among you any one that maketh his son or his daughter to pass through the fire, or that useth divination, or an observer of times, or an enchanter, or a witch.

—DEUTERONOMY 18:10

Counterattack: Bind the spirit of divination. Decree the Lordship of Christ. Pray *The Rules of Engagement, Vol. 1: The Art of Strategic Prayer and Spiritual Warfare*.

Divorce

According to 1 Corinthians 13, love is perfect. Unfortunately, we live in a less-than-perfect world with less-than-perfect people who have grand weddings but not so grand experiences within the institution of marriage. Communication suffers, a partner cheats, relationships crumble, lovers leave, or midlife happens. Divorce for some becomes the only solution for their disappointment.

Counterattack: Forgive, release, and let go of anger, depression, and bitterness. Ask God to remove feelings of resentment, betrayal, embarrassment, and loneliness. Get on with your life. Rebuild your worth and significance based on purpose and visions for a bright and better future. Take one day at a time. Take responsibility for your own life and feelings.

Doctrines of Devils

A doctrine is a rule, principle of law, or a statement of official government policy especially in foreign affairs and military strategies. Doctrines of devils therefore, are those rules, governmental policies, and principles of laws that do not adhere to or reflect biblical principles. Satan is skillful at preaching *another gospel*. The unsuspecting and innocent become easy prey because many seek to be *enlightened* rather than seek God. The New Age movement is an example of this deception.

> The light of the body is the eye: if therefore thine eye be single, thy whole body shall be full of light. But if thine eye be evil, thy whole body shall be full of darkness.

If therefore the light that is in thee be darkness, how great is that darkness!

—Matthew 6:22–23

Now the Spirit speaketh expressly, that in the latter times some shall depart from the faith, giving heed to seducing spirits, and doctrines of devils.

—1 Timothy 4:1

Counterattack: Bind the spirit of seduction. Decree and declare that truth prevails. Build prayer shields and hedges around your mind.

Doctrines of Man

As with doctrines of devils, these are principles or laws men hold and are promulgated through political policies, laws, and legislative edicts, educational curricula, religious tenets, and teachings.

But in vain they do worship me, teaching for doctrines the commandments of men.

—Matthew 15:9

Counterattack: Bind the spirit of error. Decree and declare that truth prevails.

Doubt

Doubt is characterized by feelings of uncertainty and misgivings. This was one of the weapons used against Adam and Eve in the Garden of Eden. One of the things you should never allow the enemy to cause you to doubt is the Word of God. Jesus promises us in Matthew 24:35 that "heaven and earth shall pass away, but my [His] words shall not pass away." Doubt is not necessarily a sin. But it has the power to make you sin. Doubt simply says, "I need more information." However, when doubt leads to unbelief, this is where sin enters the picture. It is never a crime to require more information, but make certain you are gaining that information from the correct source. Be careful that Satan does not seduce you into questioning the validity of the Word of God or God Himself.

> Now the serpent was more subtil than any beast of the field which the LORD God had made. And he said unto the woman, Yea, hath God said, Ye shall not eat of every tree of the garden? And the woman said unto the serpent, We may eat of the fruit of the trees of the garden: but of the fruit of the tree which is in the midst of the garden, God hath said, Ye shall not eat of it, neither shall ye touch it, lest ye die. And the serpent said unto the woman, Ye shall not surely die: for God doth know that in the day ye eat thereof, then your eyes shall be opened, and ye shall be as gods, knowing good and evil. And when the woman saw that the tree was good for food, and that it was pleasant to the eyes, and a tree to be desired to make one wise, she took of the fruit thereof, and did eat, and gave also unto her husband with her; and he did eat. And the eyes of them both were opened, and they knew that they were naked; and they sewed fig leaves together, and made themselves aprons.
>
> —GENESIS 3:1–7

For verily I say unto you, That whosoever shall say unto this mountain, Be thou removed, and be thou cast into the sea; and shall not doubt in his heart, but shall believe that those things which he saith shall come to pass; he shall have whatsoever he saith.

—MARK 11:23

Counterattack: Pray that your mind is steadfast immoveable always abounding in the work and Word of the Lord. Decrease according to 2 Thessalonians 2:2 that you are not shaken in your mind and refuse to be troubled by the attack of several spirits, and words, or any circumstance.

Enmeshments

Enmeshment has come to be a popularly-used term when speaking about codependence. The term *enmeshment* has been widely used in the family therapy literature since it was popularized by the work of Salvador Minuchin.[1] Enmeshment refers to an extreme form of proximity and intensity in family interactions which inevitably corrode and weaken boundaries that define individual autonomy until a kind of fusion occurs. This fusion creates a dysfunctional family culture which emotionally handicaps family members to a point of them not having a clear sense of self, rendering members too weak to function in an individualistic, differentiated way. Generally speaking, this condition leads a person into the position of becoming psychologically influenced, controlled by, mutually reliant upon, or needing another person to fulfill their own needs or to complete them as a person. According to Melody Beattie in her book, *Codependent No More,* enmeshment "causes people to become emotionally and psychologically consumed in a dysfunctional relationship in which they allow someone else's thoughts, opinions, emotions, and behavior to control them."[2]

> But king Solomon loved many strange women, together with the daughter of Pharaoh, women of the Moabites, Ammonites, Edomites, Zidonians, and Hittites; of the nations concerning which the LORD said unto the children of Israel, Ye shall not go in to them, neither shall they come in unto you: for surely they will turn away your heart after their gods: Solomon clave unto these in love. And he had seven hundred wives, princesses, and three hundred concubines: and his wives turned away his heart. For it came to pass, when Solomon was old, that his wives turned away his heart after other gods: and his heart was not perfect with the LORD his God, as was the heart of David his father. For Solomon went after Ashtoreth the goddess of the Zidonians, and after Milcom the abomination of the Ammonites.
>
> —1 KINGS 11:1–5

Counterattack: Break soul-ties, psychological and emotional attachments, and strongholds. Renounce codependency and declare that all present and future relationships are healthy, mutually beneficial, and interdependent.

Entanglements

When I think of the word *entangle*, I think of someone caught in a web that stagnates growth, progress, or development and keeps a person stuck in circumstances they really want to be delivered from. Entanglements can be social, relational, familial, organizational, spiritual, psychological, or financial in nature. Once God delivers you from anything, be careful because the devil will seek to cause you to fall into the same or similar entanglements again.

> For Pharaoh will say of the children of Israel, They are entangled in the land, the wilderness hath shut them in.
>
> —EXODUS 14:3

> For if after they have escaped the pollutions of the world through the knowledge of the Lord and Saviour Jesus Christ, they are again entangled therein, and overcome, the latter end is worse with them than the beginning.
>
> —2 PETER 2:20

Counterattack: Destroy entanglements. Decree and declare that Jehovah gives you the strength and courage to break free of every entanglement. "Stand fast therefore in the liberty wherewith Christ hath made us free, and be not entangled again with the yoke of bondage" (Gal. 5:1).

Ethnicities

Ethnicity relates to a particular group of people who share a common and distinctive race or linguistic, religious, or cultural heritage. Satan uses this weapon effectively to keep believers separated.

> There cometh a woman of Samaria to draw water: Jesus saith unto her, Give me to drink. (For his disciples were gone away unto the city to buy meat.)

Then saith the woman of Samaria unto him, How is it that thou, being a Jew, askest drink of me, which am a woman of Samaria? for the Jews have no dealings with the Samaritans.

—John 4:7–9

The woman saith unto him, Sir, I perceive that thou art a prophet. Our fathers worshipped in this mountain; and ye say, that in Jerusalem is the place where men ought to worship.

—John 4:19–20

Counterattack: "With all lowliness and meekness, with longsuffering, forbearing one another in love; endeavouring to keep the unity of the Spirit in the bond of peace. There is one body, and one Spirit, even as ye are called in one hope of your calling; One Lord, one faith, one baptism, One God and Father of all, who is above all, and through all, and in you all" (Eph. 4:2–6). There is neither Jew nor Greek, there is neither bond nor free, there is neither male nor female: for ye are all one in Christ Jesus" (Gal. 3:28).

Eventualities

An eventuality is a possibility of something occurring, or the consequence of an action. Eventualities operate by a law called the law of cause and effect. Satan often blinds your mind and deceives you into believing, denying, or ignoring that this principle will be suspended based on your desire or ignorance. A particular outcome may not come to pass immediately after an act that defies biblical principles, but eventually every seed sown will have its harvest. For instance, after a long period of alcoholism, a person gives their heart to the Lord only to discover, months later, that they have sclerosis of the liver. Because the individual feels that God should have healed them since they gave up the error of their ways (alcoholism), demonic spirits may seduce them into believing that God does not care and eventually they backslide. Another example is the power of the spoken word. Idle, capriciously spoken words will eventually manifest into reality. You have probably heard of a self-fulfilling prophecy. For example: "I never have money at the end of the month," then, you guessed it—when the end of the month comes you do not have money. Or: "This always happens to me," "If it ain't one thing, it's another," "I'm sick and tired of this." Eventually you will be both sick and tired.

> For they have sown the wind, and they shall reap the whirlwind.
>
> —HOSEA 8:7

> Death and life are in the power of the tongue: and they that love it shall eat the fruit thereof.
>
> —PROVERBS 18:21

> Be not deceived; God is not mocked: for whatsoever a man soweth, that shall he also reap.
>
> —GALATIANS 6:7

Counterattack: Decree and declare that God and God alone holds the key to your future: "'For I know the plans I have for you,' declares the LORD, 'plans to prosper you and not to harm you, plans to give you hope and a future'" (Jer. 29:11, NIV).

False Burdens

To be burdened for people and situations is expected of all saints, especially when it comes to the redemptive purpose of God being manifested. However, Satan wants to put false burdens upon you that cause undue stress, pressure, and discomfort. These burdens are easily distinguishable from the authentic ones in that they are heavy, often unbearable, and do not come from God. Jesus said in Matthew 11:29–30, "Take my yoke upon you, and learn of me; for I am meek and lowly in heart: and ye shall find rest unto your souls. For my yoke is easy, and my burden is light."

> For thou hast broken the yoke of his burden, and the staff of his shoulder, the rod of his oppressor, as in the day of Midian.
>
> —ISAIAH 9:4

Counterattack: Pray this verse from Isaiah, "And it shall come to pass in that day, that his burden shall be taken away from off thy shoulder, and his yoke from off thy neck, and the yoke shall be destroyed because of the anointing" (Isa. 10:27).

False Entitlement

False entitlement is a spirit that causes people to feel they deserve, have a right to, or have claim to something that is really not theirs. It could be a position, money, attention, a title, clothing, or just about anything. In the Bible, Satan used this weapon through Ahab against Naboth. Ahab wanted property that belong to Naboth and plotted and planned his demise. This spirit is relentless. It will not stop until its lust and covetousness are satiated.

And it came to pass after these things, that Naboth the Jezreelite had a vineyard, which was in Jezreel, hard by the palace of Ahab king of Samaria. And Ahab spake unto Naboth, saying, Give me thy vineyard, that I may have it for a garden of herbs, because it is near unto my house: and I will give thee for it a better vineyard than it; or, if it seem good to thee, I will give thee the worth of it in money. And Naboth said to Ahab, The LORD forbid it me, that I should give the inheritance of my fathers unto thee. And Ahab came into his house heavy and displeased because of the word which Naboth the Jezreelite had spoken to him: for he had said, I will not give thee the inheritance of my fathers. And he laid him down upon his bed, and turned away his face, and would eat no bread. But Jezebel his wife came to him, and said unto him, Why is thy spirit so sad, that thou eatest no bread? And he said unto her, Because I spake unto Naboth the Jezreelite, and said unto him, Give me thy vineyard for money; or else, if it please thee, I will give thee another vineyard for it: and he answered, I will not give thee my vineyard. And Jezebel his wife said unto him, Dost thou now govern the kingdom of Israel? arise, and eat bread, and let thine heart be merry: I will give thee the vineyard of Naboth the Jezreelite. So she wrote letters in Ahab's name, and sealed them with his seal, and sent the letters unto the elders and to the nobles that were in his city, dwelling with Naboth. And she wrote in the letters, saying, Proclaim a fast, and set Naboth on high among the people: and set two men, sons of Belial, before him, to bear witness against him, saying, Thou didst blaspheme God and the king. And then carry him out, and stone him, that he may die. And the men of his city, even the elders and the nobles who were the inhabitants in his city, did as Jezebel had sent unto them, and as it was written in the letters which she had sent unto them. They proclaimed a fast, and set Naboth on high among the people. And there came in two men, children of Belial, and sat before him: and the men of Belial witnessed against him, even against Naboth, in the presence of the people, saying, Naboth did blaspheme God and the king. Then they carried him forth out of the city, and stoned him with stones, that he died. Then they sent to Jezebel, saying, Naboth is stoned, and is dead. And it came to pass, when Jezebel heard that Naboth was stoned, and was dead, that Jezebel said to Ahab, Arise, take possession of the vineyard of Naboth the Jezreelite, which he refused to give thee for money: for Naboth is not alive, but dead. And it came to pass, when Ahab heard that Naboth was dead, that Ahab rose up to go down to the vineyard of Naboth the Jezreelite, to take possession of it.

—1 KINGS 21:1–16

Counterattack: Bind the spirit of Belial. Decree and declare you will not lose anything God has given to you in Jesus' name. Ask God to release angels to marshal and protect the boundaries and borders of all physical, spiritual, and intellectual properties and all your possessions. Build a hedge of protection around yourself personally, everything and everyone associated with you in Jesus' name.

False Expectations

This one weapon, in particular, has been used to destroy many good relationships, ministries, and organizations. Expectations are good to have, particularly those which are reasonable and those that you have for yourself. But when they encroach upon another person's freedom of choice or they are unknown to others, they can become a destructive element. Jesus lost many of His followers because they had false expectations of Him. David overcame this weapon by placing his expectations upon the Lord.

> My soul, wait thou only upon God; for my expectation is from him.
>
> —PSALM 62:5

Counterattack: Pray according to Psalm 20:7, "Some trust in chariots and some in horses, but we trust in the name of the LORD our God" (NIV). You are a God of covenant, and every promise in You is yes and no. Therefore I place my hope and faith in You and You alone. Thank You for bringing people into my life whose words and promise I can depend on.

False Impressions

The mind is a very powerful thing. The enemy, knowing its capabilities, superimposes erroneous perceptions of reality upon it. This is the weapon that was used against both Paul and Jesus by causing people to falsely perceive them.

> And he was casting out a devil, and it was dumb. And it came to pass, when the devil was gone out, the dumb

spake; and the people wondered. But some of them said, He casteth out devils through Beelzebub the chief of the devils. And others, tempting him, sought of him a sign from heaven. But he, knowing their thoughts, said unto them, Every kingdom divided against itself is brought to desolation; and a house divided against a house falleth. If Satan also be divided against himself, how shall his kingdom stand? because ye say that I cast out devils through Beelzebub. And if I by Beelzebub cast out devils, by whom do your sons cast them out? therefore shall they be your judges.

—LUKE 11:14–19

Counterattack: Pray the following prayer, "In the name of Jesus, I obliterate, annihilate, and prohibit satanic impressions, illusions, projections, perceptions, suggestions, suspicions, and deceptions set up as a decoy or an ambush to my soul and those assigned to pray with me, for me, and on behalf of me, those that work with me, are assigned to me, and interact with me daily. Amen." (See Acts 13:50; 2 Thessalonians 2:1–10; 1 King 22:5–40.)

Family Eccentricities and Idiosyncrasies

Sometimes Satan will attempt to short-circuit complete deliverance by telling us that there are certain peculiarities in our lives that give us a distinction from other individuals, like particular actions, perceptions, and behaviors that are characteristic of our family. It could be shyness or a tendency to lie or fight. It is postulated that since certain hereditary characteristics are passed down through our DNA, spirits of inheritance (demonic spirits) can attach themselves to the DNA and be passed down generationally. An example of this is Abraham and his descendants, Isaac and Jacob. They all had the proclivity to lie under pressure.

> Thou shalt not bow down thyself to them, nor serve them: for I the LORD thy God am a jealous God, visiting the iniquity of the fathers upon the children unto the third and fourth generation of them that hate me.
>
> —Exodus 20:5

> Keeping mercy for thousands, forgiving iniquity and transgression and sin, and that will by no means clear the guilty; visiting the iniquity of the fathers upon the children, and upon the children's children, unto the third and to the fourth generation.
>
> —Exodus 34:7

Counterattack: Pray, "I decree and declare that by the anointing: covenants, contracts, chains, fetters, bondages, proclivities, and captivities that are contrary to, oppose, or hinder the fulfillment of God's original plan and purpose, are broken. I am liberated from soul ties, generational, satanic, demonic alliances, allegiances, and curses or spirits of inheritance. I sever them by the blood and by the spirit. I speak to my DNA and declare that I am free from any and all influences passed down from one generation to another; biologically, socially, emotionally, physiologically, psychologically, spiritually, or by any other channel unknown to me, but known to God. I resist every spirit that acts as a doorkeeper to my soul and renounce any further conscious or unconscious alliance, association, allegiance, or covenant. I open myself to divine deliverance. Father, have your way now! Perfect those things concerning me, amen." (See Deuteronomy 5:9, 7:8–9; Ecclesiastes 7:26; Isaiah 61:1; Acts 8:9–13; Galatians 5:1; 2 Timothy 2:25; 1 Thessalonians 5:23–24.)

Fear

Fear is a powerful weapon the enemy uses against the saints. This was one of the weapons used to penetrate Job's hedge of protection. It is actually used to perforate and penetrate our faith. Fear has a diversity of expressions. (See *The Rules of Engagement, Vol. 2: Binding the Strongman* for details.)

> For the thing which I greatly feared is come upon me, and that which I was afraid of is come unto me.
>
> —JOB 3:25

> There is no fear in love; but perfect love casteth out fear: because fear hath torment. He that feareth is not made perfect in love.
>
> —1 JOHN 4:18

Counterattack: Psalm 27:1–6: "The LORD is my light and my salvation; whom shall I fear? the LORD is the strength of my life; of whom shall I be afraid? When the wicked, even mine enemies and my foes, came upon me to eat up my flesh, they stumbled and fell. Though an host should encamp against me, my heart shall not fear: though war should rise against me, in this will I be confident. One thing have I desired of the LORD, that will I seek after; that I may dwell in the house of the LORD all the days of my life, to behold the beauty of the

Lord, and to inquire in his temple. For in the time of trouble he shall hide me in his pavilion: in the secret of his tabernacle shall he hide me; he shall set me up upon a rock. And now shall mine head be lifted up above mine enemies round about me: therefore will I offer in his tabernacle sacrifices of joy; I will sing, yea, I will sing praises unto the Lord."

Fiery Darts

During biblical days, fiery darts were pointed missiles lit with fire and thrown at a target. Using this as a metaphor, Paul speaks of this weapon in Ephesians 6:16. Today, these spiritual fiery darts can be enflamed by anger, jealousy, bitterness, and rage, and require faith to counteract their effect and to protect us.

> Above all, taking the shield of faith, wherewith ye shall be able to quench all the fiery darts of the wicked.
>
> —Ephesians 6:16

Counterattack: Pray, "Father I lift up the shield of faith today and quench the fiery darts of the wicked one."

Firebrands

Firebrands were used as a type of weapon. The tail of an animal, such as a fox, would be set on fire, the animal then set loose usually in a field or through a village setting, alighting anything in its path. A firebrand can be likened to intense opposition and "heated" warfare.

He that passeth by, and meddleth with strife belonging not to him, is like one that taketh a dog by the ears. As a mad man who casteth firebrands, arrows, and death, so is the man that deceiveth his neighbour, and saith, Am not I in sport?

—PROVERBS 26:17–19

Counterattack: Pray according to this passage of Scripture, "And say unto him, Take heed, and be quiet; fear not, neither be fainthearted for the two tails of these smoking firebrands, for the fierce anger of Rezin with Syria, and of the son of Remaliah" (Isa. 7:4).

Friendly Fire

It is a fact that not all casualties of war are caused by the enemy, but sometimes by those closest to us. This is not to imply that they have malicious intent, that they are motivated to destroy us, or intentionally harm us. But they can be used by the enemy to accidentally hurt or destroy us, in spite of their sincere love for us. One of the reasons why this weapon is so powerful is the actual weapons used are their love and positive regard, rather than their hatred or ill will toward us. I have selected two examples. The first is Peter and Jesus:

Then charged he his disciples that they should tell no man that he was Jesus the Christ. From that time forth began Jesus to shew unto his disciples, how that he must go unto Jerusalem, and suffer many things of the elders and chief priests and scribes, and be killed, and be raised again the third day. Then Peter took him, and began to rebuke him, saying, Be it far from thee, Lord: this shall not be unto thee. But he turned, and said unto Peter, Get thee behind me, Satan: thou art an offence unto me: for thou savourest not the things that be of God, but those that be of men.

—MATTHEW 16:20–23

The Book of Matthew recounts where Peter, Jesus' disciple, traveling and ministerial companion, as well as close friend, is used in such a case. It is quite obvious that Peter was unaware that his love and sincere concern for Jesus could be wielded as a weapon designed to undermine the purpose of God in Jesus' life. His intention was honorable in that he wanted the best for the One whom he would eventually give his life for. Satan used this as an open door. Peter's emotional attachment to Jesus was all he needed. Had Jesus not known His purpose, been susceptible to emotional manipulation, or lacked spiritual discernment, perhaps Satan's plan might have worked. As believers, we need to be able to discern the spirit behind certain suggestions, comments, and council coming from loved ones, associates, and friends. If it does not align itself with the revealed will of God for your life, do not feel pressured to oblige.

Sometimes people are misled into believing that Satan requires insidiously motivated individuals to accomplish his tasks. This is not always the case, because his strategy would be too obvious. To accomplish anything in a person's life, particularly if that person is matured in the things of the Lord and sensitive in the Spirit, Satan will have to take a more clandestine approach in his attack against them.

The second example is with Paul and an astrologer:

And it came to pass, as we went to prayer, a certain damsel possessed with a spirit of divination met us, which brought her masters much gain by soothsaying: the same followed Paul and us, and cried, saying, These men are the servants of the most high God, which shew unto us the way of salvation. And this did she many days. But Paul, being grieved, turned and said to the spirit, I command thee in the name of Jesus Christ to come out of her. And he came out the same hour. And when her masters saw that the hope of their gains was gone, they caught Paul and Silas, and drew them into the marketplace unto the rulers, and brought them to the magistrates, saying, These men, being Jews, do exceedingly trouble our city, and teach customs, which are not lawful for us to receive, neither to observe, being Romans. And the multitude rose up together against them: and the magistrates rent off their clothes, and commanded to beat them. And when they had laid many stripes upon them, they cast them into prison, charging the jailor to keep them safely.

—ACTS 16:16–23

In this instance Paul was not associated with this demon-possessed woman, but she sought to be perceived as such. Even associates have the power to undermine the purpose of God in our lives. Of course, from this account, we are able to see that her activities were motivated and orchestrated by Satan himself. It took Paul several days before he was able to discern the spirit that was motivating what initially appeared to be gracious commendations. Had Satan accomplished his purpose, the purity of Paul's anointing and the authenticity of his apostolic ministry could have easily been brought into question, thus causing a great scandal. Paul sustained much backlash, literally and spiritually, because of the failed attempt of the enemy to destroy his reputation, ruin his influence and authority in that region, and perhaps throughout other spheres of influence.

My strong counsel to you today would be to take nothing and no one for granted. The ones we love, and the ones that love us, could very well be used to provoke us into the forfeiture of divine opportunities, ministries, and ultimately the fulfillment of purpose, maximization of potential, and reaching our destiny.

One of the reasons why I believe this particular strategy is so powerful is that we are usually more relaxed around people with whom we are close so we let our hair down, so to speak. There are four categories of people the enemy will use:

- Family (e.g. Moses, Aaron, and Miriam)

- Friends (Peter and Jesus)

- Business partners and ministerial colleagues (Paul and Barnabus)

- Confidants, counselors, and mentors (David and Ahithophel)

Counterattack: Ask God to enable you to accurately discern the spirits of man. Bind all illegal activities concerning your life. I decree and declare that a prayer shield, the anointing, and bloodline, form a hedge of protection which hides me from familiar spirits and all other demonic personalities, making it difficult if not impossible for them to effectively track or trace me in the realm of the Spirit. There shall be no perforations or penetrations. (See Job 1:7–10; Psalm 91:1–16; Exodus 12:13.)

Frustration

Frustrations result from the failure to reach some valued objective or achieve the fulfillment of purpose.

> Now when the adversaries of Judah and Benjamin heard that the children of the captivity builded the temple unto the LORD God of Israel; then they came to Zerubbabel, and to the chief of the fathers, and said unto them, Let us build with you: for we seek your God, as ye do; and we do sacrifice unto him since the days of Esar-haddon king of Assur, which brought us up hither. But Zerubbabel, and Jeshua, and the rest of the chief of the fathers of Israel, said unto them, Ye have nothing to do with us to build an house unto our God; but we ourselves together will build unto the LORD God of Israel, as king Cyrus the king of Persia hath commanded us. Then the people of the land weakened the hands of the people of Judah, and troubled them in building, and hired counsellers against them, to frustrate their purpose, all the days of Cyrus king of Persia, even until the reign of Darius king of Persia.
>
> —EZRA 4:1–5

Counterattack: Release the spirit of Nehemiah upon you. Declare and decree success and progress in Jesus' name.

Generational Curses

So many Christians misunderstand the term *curse*. According to Scripture, a generational curse is the natural outcome of an act of defiant disobedience passed down from one generation to another. These are the spirits associated with generational curses:

- Family and community peculiarities
- Eccentricities
- Social/ethnic traits, tendencies, and oddities
- Pathological conditions of mind and body
- Individualities (DNA)
- Passions
- Motives
- Intentions
- Agendas
- Habits
- Ideologies
- Perceptions
- Temperaments
- Personalities
- Illness
- Degenerative/congenital diseases

Behold, I set before you this day a blessing and a curse; a blessing, if ye obey the commandments of the LORD your God, which I command you this day: and a curse, if ye will not obey the commandments of the LORD your God, but turn aside out of the way which I command you this day, to go after other gods, which ye have not known.

—DEUTERONOMY 11:26–28

I the LORD thy God am a jealous God, visiting the iniquity of the fathers upon the children unto the third and fourth generation.

—EXODUS 20:5

The LORD is longsuffering, and of great mercy, forgiving iniquity and transgression, and by no means clearing the guilty, visiting the iniquity of the fathers upon the children unto the third and fourth generation.

—NUMBERS 14:18

Counterattack: Break generational curses in Jesus' name. Live a life of obedience. "Therefore if any man be in Christ, he is a new creature: old things are passed away; behold, all things are become new" (2 Cor. 5:17).

Gossip

Satan has been characterized as a snake. If Satan's characteristic is that of a snake, then gossip can be likened to the venom of a snake. This weapon is made powerful because it uses rumor, hearsay, sensationalized talking, and commentary to undermine and destroy a person's image, influence, reputation, relationships, name, and even future. In my opinion, this weapon has been the cause of more destruction than all wars combined! James writes in James 3:5–6, "Even so the tongue is a little member, and boasteth great things. Behold, how great a matter a little fire kindleth! And the tongue is a fire, a world of iniquity: so is the tongue among our members, that it defileth the whole body, and setteth on fire the course of nature; and it is set on fire of hell." Jesus warns us about the misuse of the tongue and the eternal judgment that awaits individuals who refuse to bring their tongue under the subjection of the lordship of Christ. He states in Matthew 12:36–37, "But I say unto you, That every idle word that men shall speak, they shall give account thereof in the day of judgment. For by thy words thou shalt be justified, and by thy words thou shalt be condemned."

Surely the serpent will bite without enchantment; and a babbler is no better.

—Ecclesiastes 10:11

And withal they learn to be idle, wandering about from house to house; and not only idle, but tattlers also and busybodies, speaking things which they ought not.

—1 Timothy 5:13

Counterattack: "Lord, how are they increased that trouble me! many are they that rise up against me. Many there be which say of my soul, There is no help for him in God. Selah. But thou, O Lord, art a shield for me; my glory, and the lifter up of mine head. I cried unto the Lord with my voice, and he heard me out of his holy hill. Selah. I laid me down and slept; I awaked; for the Lord sustained me. I will not be afraid of ten thousands of people, that have set themselves against me round about. Arise, O Lord; save me, O my God: for thou hast smitten all mine enemies upon the cheek bone; thou hast broken the teeth of the ungodly. Salvation belongeth unto the Lord: thy blessing is upon thy people. Selah" (Ps. 3:1–8). "Let the words of my mouth, and the meditation of my heart, be acceptable in thy sight, O Lord, my strength, and my redeemer" (Ps. 19:14).

Guilt

Guilt is caused when a particular principle is violated or a law broken. We also tend to feel guilty when we have not lived up to expectations and standards that we have set for ourselves. If we believe that we "should" have behaved differently or we "ought" to have done better, we likely will feel guilty. Although genuine guilt is a healthy emotion, Satan can pervert it by turning it from a remorseful awareness of having done something wrong to self-reproach. When this happens, we know that Satan has perverted a healthy emotion into a deadly weapon. When guilt assails you, rather than wallowing in your guilt to the point of defeat, pray a prayer similar to Psalm 51:1–12. Overcoming guilt and shame does not mean not caring about your actions. It involves taking responsibility for what you did and coming to terms with it. There are five steps:

> Have mercy upon me, O God, according to thy lovingkindness: according unto the multitude of thy tender mercies blot out my transgressions. Wash me throughly from mine iniquity, and cleanse me from my sin. For I acknowledge my transgressions: and my sin is ever before me. Against thee, thee only, have I sinned, and done this evil in thy sight: that thou mightest be justified when thou speakest, and be clear when thou judgest. Behold, I was shapen in iniquity; and in sin did my mother conceive me. Behold, thou desirest truth in the inward parts: and in the hidden part thou shalt make me to know wisdom. Purge me with hyssop, and I shall be clean: wash me, and I shall be whiter than snow. Make me to hear joy and

gladness; that the bones which thou hast broken may rejoice. Hide thy face from my sins, and blot out all mine iniquities. Create in me a clean heart, O God; and renew a right spirit within me. Cast me not away from thy presence; and take not thy holy spirit from me. Restore unto me the joy of thy salvation; and uphold me with thy free spirit.

Counterattack: Determine to take personal responsibility for recognizing your shortcomings. Ask God for forgiveness, forgive yourself, and make reparations where necessary.

Habits

Habits are unconscious patterns of behavior that are acquired by frequent repetition of a thought, action, or reaction, and which establish a disposition of the mind, character, or mannerism. When a behavior is practiced, day after day, you will naturally train yourself to form habits. As you regularly perform this habit you become skilled at your behavior. It becomes easy and comfortable for you to take this action over and over again. Ultimately, you begin performing this action automatically. This action has now become your routine behavior. Habitual behaviors can be beneficial and liberating to you because of your ability to perform these tasks without having to consciously think about your every action. Habits can also be destructive. They can limit our effectiveness, stunt our personal growth, cut years from our lives, create antagonistic dynamics in relationships, alienate loved ones, and basically corrode a good quality of life. Bad habits can be likened to playing Russian roulette: disaster is always imminent.

> While they promise them liberty, they themselves are the servants of corruption: for of whom a man is overcome, of the same is he brought in bondage.
>
> —2 PETER 2:19

Counterattack: Practice self-discipline. Enlist the support of family and friends by sharing with them. This one act of public accountability will make it more difficult to back out or compromise. Enlist a partner when possible. Ecclesiastes 4:9 states, "Two are better than one; because they have a good reward for their labour." Focus on the end reward and have fun. It is so much easier to form a new habit if it is perceived as enjoyable. Be prepared to reward yourself if you achieve your goal.

Harassment

Harassment is an exasperating and disturbing annoyance or irritation that threatens or undermines personal peace and tranquility. By utilizing this weapon, Satan can oppress and victimize the believer. Harassment can come in the form of verbal abuse, sexual misconduct, unrealistic demands, stalking, or continuous telephone calls. Types of harassment include:

Sexual: unwanted, unwelcomed sexual comments or actions, including touching, sexual insults, staring, unwanted "compliments" that make the target uncomfortable, and sexual rumors or innuendo.

Racial: racist comments and slurs based on skin color, language, or national origin.

Verbal: name calling, derogatory statements, bullying, insulting, or intimidation.

Religious: intolerance of someone's religious beliefs.

Ableist: insulting someone based on a real or assumed physical or mental disability.

Classist: making fun of, belittling, or demeaning someone based on socio-economic status.

Scapegoating: holding one person or group responsible for a family's, organization's, or community's problems. Isolating or rejecting a person or group of people.

> But it came to pass, that when Sanballat heard that we builded the wall, he was wroth, and took great indignation, and mocked the Jews. And he spake before his brethren and the army of Samaria, and said, What do these feeble Jews? will they fortify themselves? will they sacrifice? will they make an end in a day? will they revive the stones out of the heaps of the rubbish which are burned? Now Tobiah the Ammonite was by him, and he said, Even that which they build, if a fox go up, he shall even break down their stone wall.
>
> —Nehemiah 4:1-3

Counterattack: Pray *The Rules of Engagement, Vol. 1: The Art of Strategic Prayer and Spiritual Warfare*. Reverse, overrule, and veto every act and ill-spoken and negative word. Bind the enemy and declare Isaiah 54:17, "No weapon that is formed against thee shall prosper; and every tongue that shall rise against thee in judgment thou shalt condemn. This is the heritage of the servants of the LORD, and their righteousness is of me, saith the LORD."

Heresies

Heresies are biblical truths and doctrines contaminated by controversial or unorthodox opinions, false interpretations, and doctrines of man.

> For there must be also heresies among you, that they which are approved may be made manifest among you.
> —1 CORINTHIANS 11:19

> But there were false prophets also among the people, even as there shall be false teachers among you, who privily shall bring in damnable heresies, even denying the Lord that bought them, and bring upon themselves swift destruction.
> —2 PETER 2:1

Counterattack: Declare and decree truth prevails. Bind the spirit of deception, falsehoods, and lying.

Homosexuality

In a world where "right and wrong" often seem hard to define, and compromise has superimposed itself onto godliness and holiness according to God's standards, the issues surrounding homosexuality and sexual orientation are sometimes challenging. *Homosexuality*, in its broadest sense, is a term created by nineteenth century theorists to describe the lustful predilection, sexual orientation, and emotional interest in members of the same sex. This issue is so sensitive and so divisive that it intrinsically carries with it the potential to be offensive to everyone involved. On the one hand, the very premise of homosexual acts and orientation will be offensive to some. On the other hand, if you are a person that is of the opinion that homosexuality is acceptable, and that people should demonstrate more tolerance toward homosexuals, then you will be offended, too. The core issue here, however, is not an issue of right and wrong, but whether or not homosexual acts are acceptable in the sight of God.

At this point in my own understanding and conviction it seems to me to be an open and shut case against homosexuality. Whether a person is convinced they are born that way, it is a learned behavior, or a preference, I am convinced that it is a satanically-originated, deviant behavior used to undermine the biblical definition of family and marriage and to promote mere stimulation without the ability to procreate. Also, my presentation is not one of discussing who a person is free to love, but how that love is expressed. As with all others activities that do not please God, His grace is sufficient and His tolerant nature toward us comes loaded with His compassion to rescue our fallible human nature from its predilection to wander off. According to Romans 1:25–28, "Who changed the truth of God into a lie, and worshipped and served the creature more than the Creator, who is blessed for ever. Amen. For this cause God gave them up unto vile affections: for even their women did change the natural use into that which is against nature: and likewise also the men, leaving the natural use of the woman, burned in their lust one toward another; men with men working that which is unseemly, and receiving in themselves that recompence of their error which was meet. And even as they did not like to retain God in their knowledge, God gave them over to a reprobate mind, to do those things which are not convenient." It is important to say that my statements are not meant to offend or to judge; every person has their own challenges and one sin is no greater than the other. The point I am making and pray it will be received in the spirit given is that we serve a God who, according to Ephesians 3:20, "is able to do exceeding abundantly above all that we ask or think, according to the power that worketh in us." I pray that if you or your loved one has been held hostage by homosexuality, you would not go underground but head straight to Christ. His perfect love is sufficient to cover all. Remember that homosexuality is one of the hottest debates within the institutions of the church and government. Church-wise, debates are still prevalent as to whether practicing homosexuals will find their way to heaven. There is yet an even greater question, which is whether a homosexual will be able to live a successful kingdom-oriented life here on earth. The following scripture gives us the answer:

> Know ye not that the unrighteous shall not inherit the kingdom of God? Be not deceived: neither fornicators, nor idolaters, nor adulterers, nor effeminate, nor abusers of themselves with mankind, nor thieves, nor covetous, nor drunkards, nor revilers, nor extortioners, shall inherit the kingdom of God.
>
> —1 Corinthians 6:9–10

Counterattack: "With men it is impossible, but not with God: for with God all things are possible" (Mark 10:27). "I beseech you therefore, brethren, by the mercies of God, that ye present your bodies a living sacrifice, holy, acceptable unto God, which is your reasonable service. And be not conformed to this world: but be ye transformed by the renewing of your mind, that ye may prove what is that good, and acceptable, and perfect, will of God" (Rom. 12:1–2).

Idolatry

A deep devotion and immoderate affection of an object or a person that displaces the type of love and honor God expects from His creation.

> Confounded be all they that serve graven images, that boast themselves of idols: worship him, all ye gods.
>
> —Psalm 97:7

Counterattack: Pray Exodus 20:3, "Thou shalt have no other gods before me."

Ignorance

Ignorance is the want for knowledge in general, or in relation to a particular subject; the state of being uneducated or uninformed. It is not just the lack of knowledge that destroys, it is the lack of the need for knowledge such as the knowledge of God.

> My people are destroyed for lack of knowledge: because thou hast rejected knowledge, I will also reject thee, that thou shalt be no priest to me: seeing thou hast forgotten the law of thy God, I will also forget thy children.
>
> —Hosea 4:6

Counterattack: Ask God to give you knowledge, understanding, prudence, and wisdom. Remember Proverbs 9:10, "The fear of the LORD is the beginning of wisdom: and the knowledge of the holy is understanding."

Immaturity

Encarta offers us the following definition for the word *immaturity:* "childish: lacking the wisdom or emotional development normally associated with adults (disapproving)," such as pouting, whining, pleading, nagging, throwing tantrums, dependence, irresponsibility.

Counterattack: "But speaking the truth in love, may grow up into him in all things, which is the head, even Christ" (Eph. 4:15). "As newborn babes, desire the sincere milk of the word, that ye may grow thereby" (1 Pet. 2:2). "But grow in grace, and in the knowledge of our Lord and Saviour Jesus Christ. To him be glory both now and for ever. Amen" (2 Pet. 3:18).

Incest

Incest is defined as sexual relations between persons closely related enough that marriage would be considered illegal or forbidden. This weapon, used from the days of Lot, has been used for opening doors in many people's lives to perversion, psychotic or neurotic conditions, heinous criminal activities, and intergenerational dysfunctions.

And Lot went up out of Zoar, and dwelt in the mountain, and his two daughters with him; for he feared to dwell in Zoar: and he dwelt in a cave, he and his two daughters. And the firstborn said unto the younger, Our father is old, and there is not a man in the earth to come in unto us after the manner of all the earth: come, let us make our father drink wine, and we will lie with him, that we may preserve seed of our father. And they made their father drink wine that night: and the firstborn went in, and lay with her father; and he perceived not when she lay down, nor when she arose. And it came to pass on the morrow, that the firstborn said unto the younger, Behold, I lay yesternight with my father: let us make him drink wine this night also; and go thou in, and lie with him, that we may preserve seed of our Father. And they made their father drink wine that night also: and the younger arose, and lay with him; and he perceived not when she lay down, nor when she arose. Thus were both the daughters of Lot with child by their father. And the firstborn bare a son, and called his name Moab: the same is the father of the Moabites unto this day.

—Genesis 19:30–37

Counterattack: Read *The Rules of Engagement, Vol. 2: Binding the Strongman*. Bind the spirit of perversion. Decree and declare that the family line is cleansed from all perversions in Jesus' name. Decree and declare that by the anointing, covenants, contracts, chains, fetters, bondages, proclivities, and captivities that are contrary to, oppose, or hinder the fulfillment of God's original plan and purpose are broken. I am liberated from soul ties, generational, satanic, and demonic alliances, allegiances, curses, and spirits of inheritance. I sever them by the blood and by the spirit. I declare that I am free from any and all influences passed down from one generation to another—biologically, socially, sexually, emotionally, physiologically, psychologically, spiritually, or by any other channel unknown to me but known to God. The blood of Jesus Christ sets me free from all soulish and carnal predilections and predispositions of the flesh, and cleanses my body, soul, and spirit of all psychic and generational contaminates. I resist every spirit that acts as a doorkeeper to my soul and renounce any further conscious or unconscious alliance, association, allegiance, or covenant. I open myself to divine deliverance. Father, have your way now! Perfect those things concerning me. (See Deuteronomy 5:9, 7:8–9; Ecclesiastes 7:26; Isaiah 61:1; Acts 8:9–13; Galatians 5:1; 2 Timothy 2:25; 1 Thessalonians 5:23–24.)

Indifference

Indifference causes hope, purpose, and vision to be replaced by apathy. According to Nobel Prize-winning author Elie Wiesel, "The opposite of love is not hate, it's indifference. The opposite of art is not ugliness, it is indifference. The opposite of faith is not heresy, it is indifference. And the opposite of life is not death, it is [the failure to value life brought on by one thing only]—indifference" (paraphrase mine).[1]

> By the rivers of Babylon, there we sat down, yea, we
> wept, when we remembered Zion. We hanged our harps
> upon the willows in the midst thereof. For there they
> that carried us away captive required of us a song; and

they that wasted us required of us mirth, saying, Sing us one of the songs of Zion. How shall we sing the Lord's song in a strange land?

—Psalm 137:1–4

Counterattack: Ask God to restore the joy of your salvation to give you a zeal for life and living.

Inhibitions

Intrinsic, extrinsic, conscious, or unconscious things that prevent, restrain, block, or suppress.

And it came to pass, that as he was come nigh unto Jericho, a certain blind man sat by the way side begging: and hearing the multitude pass by, he asked what it meant. And they told him, that Jesus of Nazareth passeth by. And he cried, saying, Jesus, thou Son of David, have mercy on me. And they which went before rebuked him, that he should hold his peace: but he cried so much the more, Thou Son of David, have mercy on me.

—Luke 18:35–39

Counterattack: Pray, "I prevail against satanic inhibitions, prohibitions, and all limitations. I decree and declare that all invisible and invincible walls are destroyed." (See Colossians 1:16.)

Iniquity

Using the analogy of a tree, iniquity is to sin as the root of a tree is to the fruit. Iniquity comes from the Hebrew word *avon* and literally means "to make crooked, perverse, twisted, corrupt, and immoral." In many religious circles, it is recognized as the bedrock of generational curses.

> The LORD is longsuffering, and of great mercy, forgiving iniquity and transgression, and by no means clearing the guilty, visiting the iniquity of the fathers upon the children unto the third and fourth generation. Pardon, I beseech thee, the iniquity of this people according unto the greatness of thy mercy, and as thou hast forgiven this people, from Egypt even until now.
>
> —NUMBERS 14:18–19

> It may be that the house of Judah will hear all the evil which I purpose to do unto them; that they may return every man from his evil way; that I may forgive their iniquity and their sin.
>
> —JEREMIAH 36:3

Counterattack: Pray Psalm 32:5, "I acknowledged my sin unto thee, and mine iniquity have I not hid. I said, I will confess my transgressions unto the LORD; and thou forgavest the iniquity of my sin. Selah."

Insecurity

Insecurities create a condition that is physically or psychologically unstable, emotionally uncertain, and is marked by a lacking in confidence in one's ability, purpose, and potential. Insecurities often show up, for example, when we are in the midst of someone we perceive to be better, more capable, talented, educated, or attractive than we perceive ourselves.

> Now therefore, behold, the cry of the children of Israel is come unto me: and I have also seen the oppression wherewith the Egyptians oppress them. Come now therefore, and I will send thee unto Pharaoh, that thou mayest bring forth my people the children of Israel out of Egypt. And Moses said unto God, Who am I, that I should go unto Pharaoh, and that I should bring forth the children of Israel out of Egypt? And he said, Certainly I will be with thee; and this shall be a token unto thee, that I have sent thee: When thou hast brought forth the people out of Egypt, ye shall serve God upon this mountain.
>
> —Exodus 3:9–12

Counterattack: "For it is God which worketh in you both to will and to do of his good pleasure" (Phil. 2:13). Rely on the enabling power of the Holy Spirit, for the Spirit in you is far stronger than anything in the world. (See 1 John 4:4.)

Insults

An insult can be defined as the abasement, belittlement, degradation, and verbalization of a low opinion of something or someone. The power of an insult should not be underestimated because it has the innate ability of having a long-term effect long after it has been experienced, such as fear, anxiety, depression, low self-esteem, poor self-image, and erosion of confidence. They can take on the form of swearing, stereotyping, prejudice, racial slurs, off-color jokes, generalizations, accusations, negative personal assessments, blasphemy, inappropriate behavior, or unintentional or intentional breach of protocol. There are four types of insults:

Pragmatic: methodically delivered so as to offend, humiliate, provoke, scapegoat, or hurt deeply.

Cathartic: hostile venting of emotions.

Overt: opinions, feelings, perceptions, or verbal confrontations intended and perceived by both parties.

Covert/passive-aggressive: "sink in later" insults.

> The spirit of a man will sustain his infirmity; but a wounded spirit who can bear?
>
> —PROVERBS 18:14

Counterattack: Pray, "I obliterate and annihilate satanic impressions, insults, prejudice, harrassments, projections, perceptions, suggestions, suspicions, and deceptions set up as a decoy or an ambush to my soul and those assigned to pray with me, for me, on behalf of me, those that work with me, are assigned to me, and interact with me daily." (See Acts 13:50; 2 Thessalonians 2:1–10; 1 King 22:5–40.) Build prayer hedges and firewalls around your mind, will, and emotions. I overrule and overthrow according to Isaiah 54:17, ill-spoken words, ill wishes, enchantments, curses, and every idle word spoken contrary to God's original plans and purpose. I reverse the effects associated with these insults and decree that they shall not stand, they shall not come to pass, *they shall not take root.* Their violent verbal dealings are returned to them doublefold. Amen."

Interference

This is a satanic act or instance of hindering, impeding, or obstructing God's work and the fulfillment of destiny and purpose.

> Now when the adversaries of Judah and Benjamin heard that the children of the captivity builded the temple unto the LORD God of Israel; then they came to Zerubbabel, and to the chief of the fathers, and said unto them, Let us build with you: for we seek your God, as ye do; and we do sacrifice unto him since the days of Esar-haddon king of Assur, which brought us up hither. But Zerubbabel, and Jeshua, and the rest of the chief of the fathers of Israel, said unto them, Ye have nothing to do with us to build an house unto our God; but we ourselves together will build unto the LORD God of Israel, as king Cyrus the king of Persia hath commanded us. Then the people of the land weakened the hands of the people of Judah, and troubled them in building, and hired counsellers against them, to frustrate their purpose, all the days of Cyrus king of Persia, even until the reign of Darius king of Persia. And in the reign of Ahasuerus, in the beginning of his reign, wrote they unto him an accusation against the inhabitants of Judah and Jerusalem.
>
> —EZRA 4:1–6

Counterattack: Ask God for supernatural intervention. Pray *The Rules of Engagement, Vol. 1: The Art of Strategic Prayer and Spiritual Warfare.*

Invincible Obstructions

Since perception is everything Satan will attempt to affect our perception of what is and what is not possible. He will create a mountain out of a molehill; even though he knows that with God, nothing is impossible. In this instance, the enemy convinced an entire nation that it was not possible to overcome or defeat their obstruction. However, through the power of *Jehovah Gibbor* David overcame Goliath, the "invincible" obstruction of the nation of Israel.

And David left his carriage in the hand of the keeper of the carriage, and ran into the army, and came and saluted his brethren. And as he talked with them, behold, there came up the champion, the Philistine of Gath, Goliath by name, out of the armies of the Philistines, and spake according to the same words: and David heard them. And all the men of Israel, when they saw the man, fled from him, and were sore afraid. And the men of Israel said, Have ye seen this man that is come up? surely to defy Israel is he come up: and it shall be, that the man who killeth him, the king will enrich him with great riches, and will give him his daughter, and make his father's house free in Israel. And David spake to the men that stood by him, saying, What shall be done to the man that killeth this Philistine, and taketh away the reproach from Israel? for who is this uncircumcised Philistine, that he should defy the armies of the living God? And the people answered him after this manner, saying, So shall it be done to the man that killeth him... And he took his staff in his hand, and chose him five smooth stones out of the brook, and put them in a shepherd's bag which he had, even in a scrip; and his sling was in his hand: and he drew near to the Philistine. And the Philistine came on and drew near unto David; and the man that bare the shield went before him. And when the Philistine looked about, and saw David, he disdained him: for he was but a youth, and ruddy, and of a fair countenance. And the Philistine said unto David, Am I a dog, that thou comest to me with staves? And the Philistine cursed David by his gods. And the Philistine said to David, Come to me, and I will give thy flesh unto the fowls of the air, and to the beasts of the field. Then said David to the Philistine, Thou comest to me with a sword, and with a spear, and with a shield: but I come to thee in the name of the LORD of hosts, the God of the armies of Israel, whom thou hast defied. This day will the LORD deliver thee into mine hand; and I will smite thee, and take thine head from thee; and I will give the carcases of the host of the Philistines this day unto the fowls of the air, and to the wild beasts of the earth; that all the earth may know that there is a God in Israel. And all this assembly shall know that the LORD saveth not with sword and spear: for the battle is the LORD's, and he will give you into our hands. And it came to pass, when the Philistine arose, and came and drew nigh to meet David, that David hasted, and ran toward the army to meet the Philistine. And David put his hand in his bag, and took thence a stone, and slang it, and smote the Philistine in his forehead, that the stone sunk into his forehead; and he fell upon his face to the earth. So David prevailed over the Philistine with a sling and with a stone, and smote the Philistine, and slew him; but there was no sword in the hand of David. Therefore David ran, and stood upon the Philistine, and took his sword, and drew it out of the sheath thereof, and slew him, and cut off his head therewith. And when the Philistines saw their champion was dead, they fled.

—1 SAMUEL 17:22–27, 40–51

Counterattack: Pray 2 Samuel 22:30, "For by thee I have run through a troop: by my God have I leaped over a wall." And pray Matthew 17:20, "If ye have faith as a grain of mustard seed, ye shall say unto this mountain, Remove hence to yonder place; and it shall remove; and nothing shall be impossible unto you."

Invisible Barriers

Invisible barriers can be emotional, psychological, spiritual, financial, racial, social, national, regional, global, parochial, or political in nature. The story of Simon the sorcerer demonstrates two categories under which these weapons function:

Extrinsic

Satan skillfully uses a variety of external forces to obstruct, delay, and frustrate the plans and purpose of God. Examples of these forces are:

- Cultural limitations
- Traditions
- Political legislation
- Religious practices

- Social rituals
- Witchcraft
- Economic oppression
- Miseducation

Intrinsic

Satan also uses a variety of internal forces, emotions, and attitudes. Examples include:

- Fear
- Doubt
- Habits
- Iniquities
- Prejudices
- Perceptions
- Attitudes
- Ignorance
- Pride
- Selp-deception
- Codependence

Then Philip went down to the city of Samaria, and preached Christ unto them. And the people with one accord gave heed unto those things which Philip spake, hearing and seeing the miracles which he did. For unclean spirits, crying with loud voice, came out of many that were possessed with them: and many taken with palsies, and that were lame, were healed. And there was great joy in that city. But there was a certain man, called Simon, which beforetime in the same city used sorcery, and bewitched the people of Samaria, giving out that himself was some great one: to whom they all gave heed, from the least to the greatest, saying, This man is the great power of God. And to him they had regard, because that of long time he had bewitched them with sorceries. But when they believed Philip preaching the things concerning the kingdom of God, and the name of Jesus Christ, they were baptized, both men and women. Then Simon himself believed also: and when he was baptized, he continued with Philip, and wondered, beholding the miracles and signs which were done. Now when the apostles which were at Jerusalem heard that Samaria had received the word of God, they sent unto them Peter and John: who, when they were come down, prayed for them, that they might receive the Holy Ghost: (For as yet he was fallen upon none of them: only they were baptized in the name of the Lord Jesus.) Then laid they their hands on them, and they received the Holy Ghost. And when Simon saw that through laying on of the apostles' hands the Holy Ghost was given, he offered them money, saying, Give me also this power, that on whomsoever I lay hands, he may receive the Holy Ghost. But Peter said unto him, Thy money perish with thee, because thou hast thought that the gift of God may be purchased with money. Thou hast neither part nor lot in this matter: for thy heart is not right in the sight of God. Repent therefore of this thy wickedness, and pray God, if perhaps the thought of thine heart may be forgiven thee. For I perceive that thou art in the gall of bitterness, and in the bond of iniquity. Then answered Simon, and said, Pray ye to the Lord for me, that none of these things which ye have spoken come upon me. And they, when they had testified and preached the word of the Lord, returned to Jerusalem, and preached the gospel in many villages of the Samaritans.

—ACTS 8:5–25

Counterattack: "Every valley shall be filled, and every mountain and hill shall be brought low; and the crooked shall be made straight, and the rough ways shall be made smooth" (Luke 3:5). Employ the anointing of Zerubbabel and prophesy grace to every mountain. (See Zechariah 4:6–7.)

Irritations

The old English word for irritation is *vex*. Irritations are things that get under your skin and can be likened to an annoying fly buzzing around you. Psychological and physical in nature, an irritation is characterized by any stimulus that produces a state of annoyance which distracts one from focus and conscious thinking. It can also give rise to frustration, anger, offense, resentment, and bad feelings. Irritations are very subjective and are predicated on an individual's tolerance level and ability to focus and concentrate. Examples of this are: people talking behind you at a movie, a waitress mixing up your order, tardiness, nagging, skin irritations, etc.

> Vex the Midianites, and smite them: for they vex you with their wiles, wherewith they have beguiled you in the matter of Peor, and in the matter of Cozbi, the daughter of a prince of Midian, their sister, which was slain in the day of the plague for Peor's sake.
>
> —Numbers 25:17–18

Counterattack: Ask God to remove the irritations, or to provide divine inoculations.

Jealousy

Jealousy is an emotion provoked by any perceived threat to a relationship. Most people use the word *jealousy* interchangeably with envy. However, there is a difference. Jealousy stems from insecurity, a sense of ownership, or obsession. A jealous person usually does not want anyone else to share what or who they "possess." Conversely, envy causes a person to covet the possession of another. Jealousy may involve varying degrees of emotions such as sadness, anger, anxiety, and rage. However, many psychologists have defined jealousy as the sense of "distress" or "discomfort" experienced over a partner's real or imagined involvement with another. Even though jealousy occurs in all types of dyadic relationships, extreme cases are commonly associated with romantic relationships. It has been reported that in these extreme cases, jealousy has been known to drive people to commit heinous crimes.

> For jealousy is the rage of a man: therefore he will not spare in the day of vengeance.
>
> —PROVERBS 6:34

> Set me as a seal upon thine heart, as a seal upon thine arm: for love is strong as death; jealousy is cruel as the grave: the coals thereof are coals of fire, which hath a most vehement flame.
>
> —SONG OF SOLOMON 8:6

Counterattack: Ask God to deliver you or the person closely associated with you from the spirit of jealousy.

Judgmentalism

Judgmentalism is the inclination toward making moral judgments based on personal context and preference. People have a tendency to judge others in an attempt to force them into conformity, basically because they feel some kind of fear of their own skeletons in the closet or because what they see in others may be hidden deep within themselves.

> Speak not evil one of another, brethren. He that speaketh evil of his brother, and judgeth his brother, speaketh evil of the law, and judgeth the law: but if thou judge the law, thou art not a doer of the law, but a judge. There is one lawgiver, who is able to save and to destroy: who art thou that judgest another?
>
> —JAMES 4:11–12

Counterattack: "Judge not, and ye shall not be judged: condemn not, and ye shall not be condemned: forgive, and ye shall be forgiven" (Luke 6:37).

Lack of Spiritual Endowments

Lack of: faith, fruits of the spirit, wisdom, focus, purpose, hope, or submission falls under this category.

> Thou art weighed in the balances, and art found wanting.
>
> —DANIEL 5:27

Counterattack: Ask God to give you your spiritual inheritance and true riches in Christ Jesus. Bind the spirit of lack and speak abundance. "The young lions do lack, and suffer hunger: but they that seek the LORD shall not want

121

any good thing" (Ps. 34:10). "If any of you lack wisdom, let him ask of God, that giveth to all men liberally, and upbraideth not; and it shall be given him" (James 1:5).

Lack of Submission to Authority

Lack of submission to authority is caused by the spirits of pride and rebellion. People who do not submit to authority are self-willed, stubborn, and uninformed about the dangers associated with this kind of recalcitrant behavior. Miriam and Aaron, although close kin to Moses, were driven by this spirit and failed to fully submit to their brother Moses' leadership. This spirit led them to rebel against Moses' authority, assuming that because of the similarity in calling, office, and anointing, submission was unnecessary.

> And Miriam and Aaron spake against Moses because of the Ethiopian woman whom he had married: for he had married an Ethiopian woman. And they said, Hath the LORD indeed spoken only by Moses? Hath he not spoken also by us? And the LORD heard it.
>
> —NUMBERS 12:1–2

Counterattack: "Submit yourselves therefore to God. Resist the devil, and he will flee from you" (James 4:7). "Submit yourselves to every ordinance of man for the Lord's sake: whether it be to the king, as supreme" (1 Peter 2:13). "Likewise, ye younger, submit yourselves unto the elder. Yea, all of you be subject one to another, and be clothed with humility: for God resisteth the proud, and giveth grace to the humble" (1 Peter 5:5).

Laziness

The enemy is aware that this powerful weapon often goes undetected because it does not appear demonic at first blush. Slothfulness and inactivity leads to poverty, a lack of fulfillment of purpose, and impotence. The old-timers used to say that idleness is the "devil's workshop."

> The slothful man saith, There is a lion in the way; a lion is in the streets. As the door turneth upon his hinges, so doth the slothful upon his bed. The slothful hideth his hand in his bosom; it grieveth him to bring it again to his mouth.
>
> —Proverbs 26:13–15

Counterattack: "The hand of the diligent shall bear rule: but the slothful shall be under tribute" (Prov. 12:24). "Love not sleep, lest thou come to poverty; open thine eyes, and thou shalt be satisfied with bread" (Prov. 20:13).

Lies

Lies are false declarations, distorted facts, and fabricated statements used to deceive or give an incorrect perception. The Greek word for lie is *pseudologos*, where *pseudo* means "false" and *logos* means "word or declaration."

> Now the Spirit speaketh expressly, that in the latter times some shall depart from the faith, giving heed to seducing spirits, and doctrines of devils; Speaking lies in hypocrisy; having their conscience seared with a hot iron.
>
> —1 Timothy 4:1–2

Counterattack: "And ye shall know the truth, and the truth shall make you free" (John 8:32). Bind the spirit's lies, falsehood, and error and loose them from their assignment. Decree and declare that truth prevails.

Lusts

Lust can be defined as a strong desire of the flesh, and the desires, appetites, and cravings of the soul. To the believer, lust is the cancer of the soul. It produces leanness of the soul so that after it has completed its assignment, according to the apostle James, it brings sin and then death.

> But every man is tempted, when he is drawn away of his own lust, and enticed. Then when lust hath conceived, it bringeth forth sin: and sin, when it is finished, bringeth forth death.
>
> —JAMES 1:14–15

> This I say then, Walk in the Spirit, and ye shall not fulfil the lust of the flesh....Now the works of the flesh are manifest, which are these; Adultery, fornication, uncleanness, lasciviousness, idolatry, witchcraft, hatred, variance, emulations, wrath, strife, seditions, heresies, envyings, murders, drunkenness, revellings, and such like: of the which I tell you before, as I have also told you in time past, that they which do such things shall not inherit the kingdom of God.
>
> —GALATIANS 5:16, 19–21

For all that is in the world, the lust of the flesh, and the lust of the eyes, and the pride of life, is not of the

Father, but is of the world.

—1 John 2:16

For when they speak great swelling words of vanity, they allure through the lusts of the flesh, through much wantonness, those that were clean escaped from them who live in error.

—2 Peter 2:18

Counterattack: Pray Galatians 5:16, "This I say then, Walk in the Spirit, and ye shall not fulfil the lust of the flesh."

Manipulation

Manipulation is the employment of shrewd or devious activities and tactics in an attempt to take advantage of another. It is not only used to dominate or control, but to subtly, underhandedly, or deceptively hide true intentions. Even though manipulation involves a variety of maneuvers, tactics, and ploys, a person who is skilled in this behavior will avoid any overt display of aggression while simultaneously intimidating, bamboozling, and cajoling or coercing others into giving them what they want. Covert activities are most often the vehicle used for interpersonal manipulation. Insecure people or people with power are prime targets for satanic manipulations. In the first instance, Satan wants insecure people to feel more powerless and in the second instance Satan wants to usurp power from the powerful. Types of manipulation include:

Verbal: Innuendo, fear, name-calling, flattery, rationalization, avoidance, nagging, crying, screaming.

Relational: whining, coercion, ultimatums, bullying, and victimization.

Social: propaganda, media and printed materials, half-truths, white lies, false advertisement, covert oppression/control.

Counterattack: "Finally, my brethren, be strong in the Lord, and in the power of his might. Put on the whole armour of God, that ye may be able to stand against the wiles of the devil. For we wrestle not against flesh and blood, but against principalities, against powers, against the rulers of the darkness of this world, against spiritual wickedness in high places. Wherefore take unto you the whole armour of God, that ye may be able to withstand in the evil day, and having done all, to stand. Stand therefore, having your loins girt about with truth, and having on the breastplate of righteousness; and your feet shod with the preparation of the gospel of peace; above all, taking the shield of faith, wherewith ye shall be able to quench all the fiery darts of the wicked. And take the helmet of salvation, and the sword of the Spirit, which is the word of God: praying always with all prayer and supplication in the Spirit, and watching thereunto with all perseverance and supplication for all saints" (Eph. 6:10–18).

Materialism

Materialism is the theory or doctrine that physical well-being and worldly possessions constitute the greatest good and highest value in life. The following terms and phrases best describe and define materialism: wealth seeking, prefers extravagance and opulence, self-centered, self-seeking, superficial, believes the bigger the paycheck the more important the person, competitive, selfish, preoccupied with money, sense of entitlement, pride, comparison, competitive, image is everything, seeks status and power relative to peers/colleagues, will marry for money, cost equates with value, looks down their nose at others, prejudiced opinions, disdains financial insecurity, avoids losing status and control, looking good is more important than comfort, believes in success through appearances, status-seeking, buys status symbols, second place is not good enough, manipulative, has a need for applause, center of attention, not generous, loves to win awards, does things primarily for own benefit, gets angry when they don't get what they want, used to getting their way, prefers instant gratification.

> For what shall it profit a man, if he shall gain the whole world, and lose his own soul?
>
> —MARK 8:36

Counterattack: Pray this passage, "But seek ye first the kingdom of God, and his righteousness; and all these things shall be added unto you" (Matt. 6:33).

Miseducation

Education, the development of understanding, must be distinguished from training, the development of skill. Education in its purest sense is designed to empower individuals to fulfill purpose and maximize potential. Therefore, miseducation is its antithesis. Modern education has been legislatively subverted into training, with precious taxpayer's dollars being squandered to produce skilled individuals whose educational experience has stripped them of eleven essential elements of success and prosperity. These elements produce healthy, emotionally stable, economically empowered, contributing members of any society. They are:

- Creative thinking
- Self-awareness
- Life-skills: principle-driven and motivated, as opposed to raw survival skills
- Interpersonal skills
- Crisis management
- Spiritual awareness
- Self-discipline
- Resource management
- Problem-solving skills (vs. victimization)
- Critical consciousness: miseducation is responsible for the construction of an artificial consciousness held together by media propaganda at the expense of an authentic critical consciousness which gives an individual the ability to perceive truth from error, to resist systemic, social, political, psychological, religious, or economic oppression and to take action against tyrannical, autocratic, iron-fisted elements within a society controlled by the prince of the power of the air who, according to 2 Corinthians 4:4, blinds the minds of people.
- Critical thinking: retention and retrieval of information, establishing the relationship between word and meaning, thought and language, reasoning, analyzing, synthesizing, judging, and evaluating.

In my research, I came across the following disturbing quote which almost proves deliberate efforts are made to miseducate entire populations:

> In our dream, we have limitless resources and the people yield themselves with perfect docility to our molding hand. The present educational conventions fade from our minds, and unhampered by tradition, we work our own good will upon a grateful and responsive folk. We shall not try to make these people or any of their children into philosophers or men of learning or science. We are not to raise up from among them authors, orators, poets, or men of letters. We shall not search for embryos of great artists, painters, or musicians. Nor will we cherish even the humbler ambition to raise up from among them lawyers, doctors, preachers, politicians, statesmen, of which we now have ample supply.[1]
>
> —Frederick Gates, 1913
> Director of Charity
> Rockefeller Foundation

To state more clearly, the secular educational system is designed to separate the masses into two classes: the elite minority who become the ruling class, and the brainwashed, nonthinking working class. According to Ephesians 4:14, they are "tossed to and fro, and carried about with every wind of doctrine, by the sleight of men, and cunning craftiness, whereby they lie in wait to deceive."

If this statement is true, than miseducation is an elaborately crafted, satanically-imposed, anti-intellectual plan supported by governments (perhaps in some cases ignorantly and in others consensually) to train a skilled-based (not intellectually stimulated) people to work to create wealth for others to enjoy. Since the wealth of the sinner is laid up for the just, we need to be reeducated in order to materialize the next great wealth transfer.

Perhaps the best way to grasp this diabolical weapon is to examine two quotes and the story of Helen Keller.

As a blind and deaf child, Helen lived much like an animal, rushing from one sensation to another. She was trained to be animalistic, a person surviving a disability, rather than educated to be a person living with a disability, until Anne Mansfield Sullivan was introduced into her world. Within a short period of becoming Helen's teacher, Sullivan was able to impart the concept of language to her, leaving only one educational mountain left to conquer which held the secret to unlocking Helen's potential hidden beneath her disability: comprehension and the awakening to *meaning*. The turning point was when Helen saw the correlation between the water that slipped through her fingers and the word *water* she had been repeating. This simple but life-altering event made it possible for Helen to begin understanding instead of simply repeating what Anne was teaching her. Helen had been trained to repeat the word *water*, but it wasn't until she combined the experience of feeling water and trying to communicate the word *water* simultaneously that Helen gained the wonderful gift of meaning and comprehension of language. These two elements, once kept from the education process, will keep a group of people unconsciously oppressed, and believing that their oppressed state is normal. Up to that point, Helen had been like a well-trained animal, memorizing words, speaking them, and receiving praise from Anne. But now, suddenly, it came to her! The word *water* actually *referred to*, *pointed to*, *meant* the exuberant liquid that ran through her fingers.

So the true and greatest casualty of spiritual warfare is not the human body, but the human mind. This is perhaps the greatest travesty of this weapon of mass destruction, the demise of the human soul.

Counterattack: "Don't become so well-adjusted to your culture that you fit into it without even thinking. Instead, fix your attention on God. You'll be changed from the inside out. Readily recognize what he wants from you, and quickly respond to it. Unlike the culture around you, always dragging you down to its level of immaturity, God brings the best out of you, develops well-formed maturity in you" (Rom. 12:2, MSG). "For though we walk in the flesh, we do not war after the flesh: (for the weapons of our warfare are not carnal, but mighty through God to the pulling down of strong holds;) Casting down imaginations, and every high thing that exalteth itself against the knowledge of God, and bringing into captivity every thought to the obedience of Christ; and having in a readiness to revenge all disobedience, when your obedience is fulfilled" (2 Cor. 10:3–6). "But grow in grace, and in the knowledge of our Lord and Saviour Jesus Christ. To him be glory both now and for ever. Amen" (2 Pet. 3:18).

Misfortunes

Misfortunes are circumstances that bring calamity, hardship, and difficult and challenging times. This weapon has a variety of faces, namely:

- Untimely Deaths
- Loss of Income

- Accidents
- Economic Hardship

Now there cried a certain woman of the wives of the sons of the prophets unto Elisha, saying, Thy servant my husband is dead; and thou knowest that thy servant did fear the LORD: and the creditor is come to take unto him my two sons to be bondmen.

—2 KINGS 4:1

Counterattack: See *The Rules of Engagement, Vol. 1: The Art of Strategic Prayer and Spiritual Warfare* for further prayer study on this topic.

Mistrust

Mistrust is a feeling of uncertainty about a situation or misgivings about a person or organization.

And it came to pass, when he had made an end of speaking unto Saul, that the soul of Jonathan was knit with the soul of David, and Jonathan loved him as his own soul. And Saul took him that day, and would let him go no more home to his father's house. Then Jonathan and David made a covenant, because he loved him as his own soul. And Jonathan stripped himself of the robe that was upon him, and gave it to David, and his garments, even to his sword, and to his bow, and to his girdle. And David went out whithersoever Saul sent him, and behaved himself wisely: and Saul set him over the men of war, and he was accepted in the sight of all the people, and also in the sight of Saul's servants. And it came to pass as they came, when David was returned from the slaughter of the Philistine, that the women came out of all cities of Israel, singing and dancing, to meet king Saul, with tabrets, with joy, and with instruments of musick. And the women answered one another as they played, and said, Saul hath slain his thousands, and David his ten thousands. And Saul was very wroth, and the saying displeased him; and he said, They have ascribed unto David ten thousands, and to me they have ascribed but thousands: and what can he have more but the kingdom? And Saul eyed David from that day and forward.

—1 SAMUEL 18:1–9

Counterattack: Ask God to reveal the intent and content of a person's heart. Discern the spirit of those operating around you and interacting with you. Ask God to make you more trusting.

Moving Out of the Timing of the Lord

This is a powerful weapon used against individuals called into ministry. Through a strong satanic provocation both David and Saul moved out of the timing of the Lord much to the detriment of their destinies. We read in 1 Samuel how the internal pressures of insecurity were used as an intrinsic weapon to cause Saul to disregard the Lord's call to wait. In the case of David, although it was his kingly responsibility to conduct a census of the people, it was not in the timing of the Lord. Hence, not only were there severe personal consequences, but an entire nation was affected. As we wait on God for our ministry we must also remember that since our times and seasons are in the hand of the Lord, there is no need to be anxious for, rushed, or hurried in the maturation process through impatience or satanic provocation. (See Romans 12:7.)

> And Satan stood up against Israel, and provoked David to number Israel.
>
> —1 CHRONICLES 21:1

Counterattack: Ask God to allow you to move in the anointing of the Sons of Isaachar so that you will discern the proper time and season for all things. Decree and declare that you are synchronized and syncopated to the timing of the Lord, moving in His will and with the prophetic "cloud."

Negativity

Circumstances, situations, and people may sometimes appear as if they have no positive characteristic or value. Sometimes our judgments are based on past experience or irrational thoughts. Negativity alters the perception of an individual and causes them to remove the colorful dynamics of life and the world and paints them gray and grim. Negativity does not only alter a person's present life, it alters their future. According to Numbers 14, one day of negativity has the power to take a person into a year's worth of bondage. Sustained negativity changes a person's mood, affects their relationships, and suppresses their immune system.

And the LORD spake unto Moses and unto Aaron, saying, how long shall I bear with this evil congregation, which murmur against me? I have heard the murmurings of the children of Israel, which they murmur against me. Say unto them, As truly as I live, saith the LORD, as ye have spoken in mine ears, so will I do to you: your carcases shall fall in this wilderness; and all that were numbered of you, according to your whole number, from twenty years old and upward, which have murmured against me, doubtless ye shall not come into the land, concerning which I sware to make you dwell therein, save Caleb the son of Jephunneh, and Joshua the son of Nun. But your little ones, which ye said should be a prey, them will I bring in, and they shall know the land which ye have despised. But as for you, your carcases, they shall fall in this wilderness. And your children shall wander in the wilderness forty years, and bear your whoredoms, until your carcases be wasted in the wilderness. After the number of the days in which ye searched the land, even forty days, each day for a year, shall ye bear your iniquities, even forty years, and ye shall know my breach of promise.

—NUMBERS 14:26–34

Counterattack: "Finally, brethren, whatsoever things are true, whatsoever things are honest, whatsoever things are just, whatsoever things are pure, whatsoever things are lovely, whatsoever things are of good report; if there be any virtue, and if there be any praise, think on these things" (Phil. 4:8).

Nets

Nets are things Satan places in your life that lead to situations from which escape is difficult. The Internet has now become one of his modern-day weapons of choice, through which individuals have been introduced and held captive to perverted cyber-space activities.

> And I find more bitter than death the woman, whose heart is snares and nets, and her hands as bands: whoso pleaseth God shall escape from her; but the sinner shall be taken by her.
>
> —ECCLESIASTES 7:26

Counterattack: In the name of Jesus, I take the sword of the spirit and sever all nets and decree and declare whom the Son sets free is free indeed! I decree and declare that every unholy alliance and association is severed in Jesus' name.

Obsession

An obsession is a compulsive fixation upon an idea, emotion, or person. Obsessions are open doors to some of the most heinous crimes and twisted activities.

> And it came to pass after this, that Absalom the son of David had a fair sister, whose name was Tamar; and Amnon the son of David loved her. And Amnon was so vexed, that he fell sick for his sister Tamar; for she was a virgin; and Amnon thought it hard for him to do any thing to her ....And when she had brought them unto him to eat, he took hold of her, and said unto her, Come lie with me, my sister. And she answered him, Nay, my

brother, do not force me; for no such thing ought to be done in Israel: do not thou this folly....Howbeit he would not hearken unto her voice: but, being stronger than she, forced her, and lay with her.

—2 SAMUEL 13:1–2, 11–12, 14

Counterattack: Fast and pray according to Isaiah 58:5–11, "Is it such a fast that I have chosen? a day for a man to afflict his soul? is it to bow down his head as a bulrush, and to spread sackcloth and ashes under him? wilt thou call this a fast, and an acceptable day to the LORD? Is not this the fast that I have chosen? to loose the bands of wickedness, to undo the heavy burdens, and to let the oppressed go free, and that ye break every yoke? Is it not to deal thy bread to the hungry, and that thou bring the poor that are cast out to thy house? when thou seest the naked, that thou cover him; and that thou hide not thyself from thine own flesh? Then shall thy light break forth as the morning, and thine health shall spring forth speedily: and thy righteousness shall go before thee; the glory of the LORD shall be thy rereward. Then shalt thou call, and the LORD shall answer; thou shalt cry, and he shall say, Here I am. If thou take away from the midst of thee the yoke, the putting forth of the finger, and speaking vanity; and if thou draw out thy soul to the hungry, and satisfy the afflicted soul; then shall thy light rise in obscurity, and thy darkness be as the noonday: and the LORD shall guide thee continually, and satisfy thy soul in drought, and make fat thy bones: and thou shalt be like a watered garden, and like a spring of water, whose waters fail not."

Offenses

Offenses are used by Satan to cause you to transgress based on your displeasure, anger, or resentment of someone's action displayed or words spoken to or against you. When an offense is allowed to remain and fester the enemy not only uses it to destroy you or the individual, but this weapon actually undermines spiritual authority. Seek to love the Word of God, especially Scripture that speaks about forgiveness and love. The following two passages from the Bible will inoculate you from the effects of this weapon:

> Great peace have they which love thy law: and nothing shall offend them.

> —PSALM 119:165

> Then said he unto the disciples, It is impossible but that offences will come: but woe unto him, through whom they come! It were better for him that a millstone were hanged about his neck, and he cast into the sea, than that he should offend one of these little ones. Take heed to yourselves: If thy brother trespass against thee, rebuke him; and if he repent, forgive him. And if he trespass against thee seven times in a day, and seven times in a day turn again to thee, saying, I repent; thou shalt forgive him. And the apostles said unto the Lord, Increase our faith. And the Lord said, If ye had faith as a grain of mustard seed, ye might say unto this sycamine tree, Be thou plucked up by the root, and be thou planted in the sea; and it should obey you. But which of you, having a servant plowing or feeding cattle, will say unto him by and by, when he is come from the field, Go and sit down to meat? And will not rather say unto him, Make ready wherewith I may sup, and gird thyself, and serve me,

till I have eaten and drunken; and afterward thou shalt eat and drink? Doth he thank that servant because he did the things that were commanded him? I trow not. So likewise ye, when ye shall have done all those things which are commanded you, say, We are unprofitable servants: we have done that which was our duty to do.

—LUKE 17:1–10

Counterattack: "Father, I release (name the person) from all offenses I have held in my heart. Forgive me for my resentment, hatred, anger, and displeasure. Deliver me from this self-imposed bondage. Close every portal that gives the spirit of unforgiveness access to my soul. I worship you as I decree and declare that where the spirit of the Lord is there is liberty."

Oppression

According to Proverbs 28:3, this weapon is like a "sweeping rain which leaveth no food." It totally ravishes the soul and leaves it wanting as it steals your dignity and quality of life. Thank God, according to Acts 10:38, that He "anointed Jesus of Nazareth with the Holy Ghost and with power: who went about doing good, and healing all that were oppressed of the devil; for God was with him." (For further insights, see *The Rules of Engagement, Vol. 2: Binding the Strongman*).

> The people of the land have used oppression, and exercised robbery, and have vexed the poor and needy: yea, they have oppressed the stranger wrongfully.
>
> —EZEKIEL 22:29

Counterattack: "Moreover the prince shall not take of the people's inheritance by oppression, to thrust them out of their possession; but he shall give his sons inheritance out of his own possession: that my people be not scattered every man from his possession" (Ezek. 46:18).

Overt Operations

There are times when Satan's attack upon you requires a less than obvious tactic. Equally, there are other times when his attack is "in your face" and obvious. This is what we call an overt attack. It is bold and brazen, and Satan definitely wants to get the glory.

And it came to pass, when David and his men were come to Ziklag on the third day, that the Amalekites had invaded the south, and Ziklag, and smitten Ziklag, and burned it with fire; and had taken the women captives, that were therein: they slew not any, either great or small, but carried them away, and went on their way. So David and his men came to the city, and, behold, it was burned with fire; and their wives, and their sons, and their daughters, were taken captives. Then David and the people that were with him lifted up their voice and wept, until they had no more power to weep. And David's two wives were taken captives, Ahinoam the Jezreelitess, and Abigail the wife of Nabal the Carmelite. And David was greatly distressed; for the people spake of stoning him, because the soul of all the people was grieved, every man for his sons and for his daughters: but David encouraged himself in the LORD his God. And David said to Abiathar the priest, Ahimelech's son, I pray thee, bring me hither the ephod. And Abiathar brought thither the ephod to David. And David inquired at the Lord, saying, Shall I pursue after this troop? shall I overtake them? And he answered him, Pursue: for thou shalt surely overtake them, and without fail recover all.

—1 Samuel 30:1–8

Counterattack: "Finally, my brethren, be strong in the Lord, and in the power of his might. Put on the whole armour of God, that ye may be able to stand against the wiles of the devil. For we wrestle not against flesh and blood, but against principalities, against powers, against the rulers of the darkness of this world, against spiritual wickedness in high places. Wherefore take unto you the whole armour of God, that ye may be able to withstand in the evil day, and having done all, to stand. Stand therefore, having your loins girt about with truth, and having on the breastplate of righteousness; and your feet shod with the preparation of the gospel of peace; above all, taking the shield of faith, wherewith ye shall be able to quench all the fiery darts of the wicked. And take the helmet of salvation, and the sword of the Spirit, which is the word of God: praying always with all prayer and supplication in the Spirit, and watching thereunto with all perseverance and supplication for all saints" (Eph. 6:10–18).

Peer Pressure

The external pressure exerted upon an individual by colleagues, friends, and associates that psychologically affects them, causing them to fundamentally conform to a specific code of conduct, mind-set, and basic way of living. Peer pressure makes you live by the standards of man rather than that established by God. Since the word *peer* is defined as, "a person who has equal standing with another or others, as in rank, class, or age," the phrase *peer pressure* preempts the notion that this phenomenon is specific to teenagers. That is to say that no matter how young or old you are, everyone is susceptible to it.

> Wherefore then didst thou not obey the voice of the LORD, but didst fly upon the spoil, and didst evil in the sight of the LORD? And Saul said unto Samuel, Yea, I have obeyed the voice of the LORD, and have gone the way which the LORD sent me, and have brought Agag the king of Amalek, and have utterly destroyed the Amalekites. But the people took of the spoil, sheep and oxen, the chief of the things which should have been utterly destroyed, to sacrifice unto the LORD thy God in Gilgal.
>
> —1 SAMUEL 15:19–21

Counterattack: "And be not conformed to this world: but be ye transformed by the renewing of your mind, that ye may prove what is that good, and acceptable, and perfect, will of God" (Rom. 12:2).

Perversions

Perversions are any kind of action that God considers deviant, corrupt, or vile. Proverbs 17:20 states, "He that hath a froward heart findeth no good: and he that hath a perverse tongue falleth into mischief."

And there came two angels to Sodom at even; and Lot sat in the gate of Sodom: and Lot seeing them rose up to meet them; and he bowed himself with his face toward the ground; and he said, Behold now, my lords, turn in, I pray you, into your servant's house, and tarry all night, and wash your feet, and ye shall rise up early, and go on your ways. And they said, Nay; but we will abide in the street all night. And he pressed upon them greatly; and they turned in unto him, and entered into his house; and he made them a feast, and did bake unleavened bread, and they did eat. But before they lay down, the men of the city, even the men of Sodom, compassed the house round, both old and young, all the people from every quarter: and they called unto Lot, and said unto him, Where are the men which came in to thee this night? bring them out unto us, that we may know them. And Lot went out at the door unto them, and shut the door after him, and said, I pray you, brethren, do not so wickedly. Behold now, I have two daughters which have not known man; let me, I pray you, bring them out unto you, and do ye to them as is good in your eyes: only unto these men do nothing; for therefore came they under the shadow of my roof. And they said, Stand back. And they said again, This one fellow came in to sojourn, and he will needs be a judge: now will we deal worse with thee, than with them. And they pressed sore upon the man, even Lot, and came near to break the door. But the men put forth their hand, and pulled Lot into the house to them, and shut to the door. And they smote the men that were at the door of the house with blindness, both small and great: so that they wearied themselves to find the door.

—Genesis 19:1–11

Counterattack: "Be not wise in thine own eyes: fear the LORD, and depart from evil" (Prov. 3:7). Break the hold of every evil, unclean power over your life, in Jesus' name. Declare that the blood of Jesus Christ cleanses you from all sin. Ask God to remove the appetite for this sin. Break ungodly soul-ties, renounce diabolical contracts, and destroy unholy alliances. Shun the very appearance of evil. Ask the Holy Spirit to expose and destroy every stronghold and cleanse you from sexual perversions. Fill your heart and mind with the Word of the Lord and decree that godly thoughts, visions, and dreams replace immoral, degrading thoughts, dreams, nightmares, and fantasies. Decree and declare your freedom in Jesus' name. "Blessed are the pure in heart: for they shall see God" (Matt. 5:8).

Possession

Possession is the state of being ruled, controlled, and dominated by an evil spirit.

> When the even was come, they brought unto him many that were possessed with devils: and he cast out the spirits with his word, and healed all that were sick.
> —MATTHEW 8:16

> And when he was come to the other side into the country of the Gergesenes, there met him two possessed with devils, coming out of the tombs, exceeding fierce, so that no man might pass by that way.
> —MATTHEW 8:28

> Then was brought unto him one possessed with a devil, blind, and dumb: and he healed him, insomuch that

the blind and dumb both spake and saw.

—MATTHEW 12:22

And at even, when the sun did set, they brought unto him all that were diseased, and them that were possessed with devils.

—MARK 1:32

Counterattack: "And it shall come to pass in that day, that his burden shall be taken away from off thy shoulder, and his yoke from off thy neck, and the yoke shall be destroyed because of the anointing" (Isa. 10:27).

Poverty

Poverty is a state of economic deficiency characterized by the lack of capacity to obtain the basic necessities of life or material comforts. The unfortunate thing about individuals who experience poverty is that they often blame their state on the Lord, rather than the real culprit, Satan. Poverty causes a lack of access.

I went out full, and the LORD hath brought me home again empty: why then call ye me Naomi, seeing the LORD hath testified against me, and the Almighty hath afflicted me?

—RUTH 1:21

For the oppression of the poor, for the sighing of the needy, now will I arise, saith the LORD; I will set him in safety from him that puffeth at him.

—PSALM 12:5

Counterattack: Bind the spirit of poverty. Ask God to give you an open heaven, divine inspiration, and to open streams of income. Make certain you are paying your tithes and planting seeds. A seed does not necessarily have to be money. You can sow seeds of hospitality, kind deeds, and acts of service and time.

Prejudice

A preconceived preference or idea which leads to the development of adverse judgment, opinion, or belief prior to and without knowledge or examination of the facts. It is also an irrational suspicion or hatred of a particular group, race, or religion. The enemy uses this weapon to separate and divide. As it relates to the church, this weapon is employed in an attempt to undermine the preaching of the Gospel and the unity of the Spirit among believers of different ethnicities, nationalities, and denominational preferences.

On the morrow, as they went on their journey, and drew nigh unto the city, Peter went up upon the housetop to pray about the sixth hour: and he became very hungry, and would have eaten: but while they made ready, he fell into a trance, and saw heaven opened, and a certain vessel descending unto him, as it had been a great sheet knit at the four corners, and let down to the earth: wherein were all manner of fourfooted beasts of the earth, and wild beasts, and creeping things, and fowls of the air. And there came a voice to him, Rise, Peter; kill, and eat. But Peter said, Not so, Lord; for I have never eaten any thing that is common or unclean. And the voice spake unto him again the second time,

What God hath cleansed, that call not thou common.

—Acts 10:9–15

Counterattack: Pray Galatians 3:28, "There is neither Jew nor Greek, there is neither bond nor free, there is neither male nor female: for ye are all one in Christ Jesus."

Pride

Pride is to the kingdom of darkness what humility is to the kingdom of light. In fact, pride is the foundation upon which the kingdom of darkness is built. Pride is essentially a declaration of independence from God because it produces an inordinate opinion of self, and personal superiority. The spirit of pride caused Satan to believe that He could be God.

When pride cometh, then cometh shame: but with the lowly is wisdom.

—Proverbs 11:2

Pride goeth before destruction, and an haughty spirit before a fall.

—Proverbs 16:18

A man's pride shall bring him low: but honour shall uphold the humble in spirit.

—Proverbs 29:23

Counterattack: Pray these passages, "But he giveth more grace. Wherefore he saith, God resisteth the proud, but giveth grace unto the humble" (James 4:6); "Humble yourselves in the sight of the Lord, and he shall lift you up" (James 4:10).

Projections

This weapon is formed in the mind of individuals causing them to attribute their attitudes, feelings, or suppositions to another. In our text, Laban accuses Jacob of the very thing he did to Jacob during Jacob's career within his corporation. He projected his guilt onto another:

> And Jacob was wroth, and chode with Laban: and Jacob answered and said to Laban, What is my trespass? what is my sin, that thou hast so hotly pursued after me? Whereas thou hast searched all my stuff, what hast thou found of all thy household stuff? set it here before my brethren and thy brethren, that they may judge betwixt us both. This twenty years have I been with thee; thy ewes and thy she goats have not cast their young, and the rams of thy flock have I not eaten. That which was torn of beasts I brought not unto thee; I bare the loss of it; of my hand didst thou require it, whether stolen by day, or stolen by night. Thus I was; in the day the drought consumed me, and the frost by night; and my sleep departed from mine eyes. Thus have I been twenty years in thy house; I served thee fourteen years for thy two daughters, and six years for thy cattle: and thou hast changed my wages ten times. Except the God of my father, the God of Abraham, and the fear of Isaac, had been with me, surely thou hadst sent me away now empty. God hath seen mine affliction and the labour of my hands, and rebuked thee yesternight.
>
> —GENESIS 31:36–42

Counterattack: Pray, "I obliterate and annihilate satanic impressions, illusions, projections, perceptions, suggestions, suspicions, and deceptions set up as a decoy or an ambush to my soul and those assigned to pray with me, for me, on behalf of me, those that work with me, are assigned to me, and interact with me daily in Jesus' name. Amen." (See Acts 13:50; 2 Thessalonians 2:1–10; 1 Kings 22:5–40.)

Provocation

A provocation is a perturbing stimulus that intentionally incites or rouses you to actions and activities that are usually diametrically opposed to the will of God.

> And Satan stood up against Israel, and provoked David to number Israel. And David said to Joab and to the rulers of the people, Go, number Israel from Beer-sheba even to Dan; and bring the number of them to me, that I may know it. And Joab answered, The LORD make his people an hundred times so many more as they be: but, my lord the king, are they not all my lord's servants? why then doth my lord require this thing? why will he be a cause of trespass to Israel?....And God was displeased with this thing; therefore he smote Israel. And David said unto God, I have sinned greatly, because I have done this thing: but now, I beseech thee, do away the iniquity of thy servant; for I have done very foolishly.
>
> —1 CHRONICLES 21:1–3, 7–8

Counterattack: Pray that God will grant you the ability to discern the spirit of provocation whenever it is operable. Forcefully resist it in Jesus' name. Decree and declare that you are led by the Spirit of the Lord.

Rape

Rape is the violation of the physiological, psychological, and emotional self by another. It is one of the many weapons the spirit of perversion uses to destroy an individual's quality of life.

Although rape is viewed as a violent sexual crime perpetrated by males against females, statistics show that a small number of cases have been reported where the victim has been male. Nevertheless, rape is not about sex. It is more than just an act of sexual violence. It is an act of the exertion of power and control over another person. Rape is life threatening and life altering; it severely traumatizes the victim. For many victims, rape is a defining moment that divides their life into two parts: life before the rape and life after. In some measure, the same is true for those who are closest to the victim including their children and male relationships such as husbands, fathers, brothers, and male companions. For all, one single incidence of rape reshapes and remolds perceptions of self, how they interact with others, and how they and their loved ones conduct the affairs of their lives in the future.

Rape is a disturbingly frequent crime. It is also one of the least-reported crimes in part because many victims fear how they might be treated if they divulge what has happened.

Now as they were making their hearts merry, behold, the men of the city, certain sons of Belial, beset the house round about, and beat at the door, and spake to the master of the house, the old man, saying, Bring forth the man that came into thine house, that we may know him. And the man, the master of the house, went out unto them, and said unto them, Nay, my brethren, nay, I pray you, do not so wickedly; seeing that this man is come into mine house, do not this folly. Behold, here is my daughter a maiden, and his concubine; them I will bring out now, and humble ye them, and do with them what seemeth good unto you: but unto this man do not so vile a thing. But the men would not hearken to him: so the man took his concubine, and brought her forth unto them; and they knew her, and abused her all the night until the morning: and when the day began to spring, they let her go. Then came the woman in the dawning of the day, and fell down at the door of the man's house where her lord was, till it was light. And her lord rose up in the morning, and opened the doors of the house, and went out to go his way: and, behold, the woman his concubine was fallen down at the door of the house, and her hands were upon the threshold. And he said unto her, up, and let us be going. But none answered. Then the man took her up upon an ass, and the man rose up, and gat him unto his place.

—Judges 19:22–28

Counterattack: Break the silence, speak up, and speak out. Seek Christian counseling. Involve loved ones and family members in the counseling sessions. Seek a powerful, safe, accepting, and supportive climate for you to release painful feelings without fear of criticism, judgment, rejection, or humiliation. Utilize prayer strategy from *The Rules of Engagement, Vol. 1: The Art of Strategic Prayer and Spiritual Warfare*. It may seem as if you will never heal, but in your weakness and sadness God's strength is made perfect. Build prayer shields, firewalls, and prayer-hedges around your life, mind, soul, and spirit. Progress through the grieving process (psychologists offer the first five stages, but I have added the last two): denial, resentment, bargaining, depression, acceptance, regaining personal power, and living life on purpose). Through Jesus Christ there is life after death. Allow the unconditional love of the Father to heal you.

Rebellion

Rebellion is to the kingdom of darkness as righteousness, peace, and joy in the Holy Spirit is to the kingdom of light. It is the very foundation upon which Satan built his kingdom of sin and iniquity. Rebellion is a demonic disposition that leads to defiance of authority, insurrection, and violence.

> For rebellion is as the sin of witchcraft, and stubbornness is as iniquity and idolatry. Because thou hast rejected the word of the LORD, he hath also rejected thee from being king.
>
> —1 SAMUEL 15:23

Counterattack: Pray without ceasing. Bind the spirit of rebellion. Decree and declare peace, compliance, and obedience are superimposed over the spirit of rebellion.

Regret

The weapon of regret is a satanic abortive weapon because it keeps you connected to your past, rather than living for the future. Remember, yesterday is in the tomb and tomorrow is yet in the womb. Regret lead Judas to hang himself. His other option would have been confession, repentance, and restoration—three acts which had the potential of salvaging his ministry and giving him a future. Regrets led people to live with "I wish," "what if," and "if...then."

> When the morning was come, all the chief priests and elders of the people took counsel against Jesus to put him to death: And when they had bound him, they led him away, and delivered him to Pontius Pilate the governor. Then Judas, which had betrayeth him, when he saw that he was condemned, repented himself, and brought again the thirty pieces of silver to the chief priests and elders, Saying, I have sinned in that I have betrayed the innocent blood. And they said, what is that to us? see thou to that. And he cast down the pieces of silver in the temple, and departed, and went and hanged himself.
>
> —Matthew 27:1–5

Counterattack: Ask God to empower you to overcome the pain, guilt, shame, and humiliation of the past. Live life on purpose. Live life in the now. Accept forgiveness. "Forgetting the past and looking forward to what lies ahead" (Phil. 3:13).

Rejection

When God created mankind He created both male and female in His image. I believe that one of the things that makes man like God is the inherent desire to be recognized, valued, accepted, and appreciated. Rejection undermines that natural, God-given characteristic which predisposes each one of us with the desire to be loved, cherished, and appreciated not for what we do, have, or attain, but for just being an individual who has been fearfully and wonderfully made. Rejection is one of the ways the enemy undermines self-worth, self-esteem, self-image, purpose, and potential. Rejection comes in two basic forms: covert and overt. Covert can be characterized by someone saying they love and support you, but never showing it. Overt is more obvious. It comprises verbal, physical, or social ostracizing, isolation, discrimination, and segregation.

These experiences of rejection produce certain attitudes toward self, parents, loved ones, spouses, other people in general, and God. Rejection from others often leads to the rejection of self which produces feelings of worthlessness and inferiority, depression, emotional isolation, introspection, perfectionism, irresponsibility, guilt, and self-hatred. People who have lived under constant rejection eventually have a difficult time expressing feelings, asserting him/herself, or taking control of his/her life. Rejected people reject as a result of an acquired defense mechanism.

Toward parents, on the one hand, the rejected person may experience resentment, bitterness, refusal to communicate, rebellion against parental authority, ambivalence, and distrust. In essence, this person says, "You rejected me, now I will reject you." On the other hand, rejected persons may form a codependent attachment to the parents. The adult child may spend a lifetime trying to gain the acceptance and love which deep down they have always sensed is missing. Yet the person may never fully understand why there is a lack of closeness or communication in the relationship.

Rejection hurts and can cause intense pain to the one who is rejected. I have learned that people do not always reject you based on inferiority. Sometimes rejection is based on perceived superiority as well. (For a greater study, please acquire a copy of *The Rules of Engagement, Vol. 2: Binding the Strongman*.)

> And he began to teach them, that the Son of man must suffer many things, and be rejected of the elders, and of the chief priests, and scribes, and be killed, and after three days rise again.
>
> —MARK 8:31

> And have ye not read this scripture; The stone which the builders rejected is become the head of the corner.
>
> —MARK 12:10

Counterattack: Ask God to show you your true worth in Him. Do not seek affirmation from others at the expense of the affirmation that God gives you. See yourself as God sees you. "To the praise of the glory of his grace, wherein he hath made us accepted in the beloved" (Eph. 1:6).

Religiosity

A system of beliefs, principles, creeds, dogmas, and faith to which an individual adheres.

> For ye have heard of my conversation in time past in the Jews' religion, how that beyond measure I persecuted the church of God, and wasted it: And profited in the Jews' religion above many my equals in mine own nation, being more exceedingly zealous of the traditions of my fathers.
>
> —Galatians 1:13–14

> If any man among you seem to be religious, and bridleth not his tongue, but deceiveth his own heart, this man's religion is vain. Pure religion and undefiled before God and the Father is this, To visit the fatherless and widows in their affliction, and to keep himself unspotted from the world.
>
> —James 1:26–27

Counterattack: Pray Matthew 6:10, "Thy kingdom come. Thy will be done in earth, as it is in heaven."

Resentment

Resentment is an irrational mind-set created by the enemy that causes a person to feel indignation or ill will toward another as a result of a real or imagined grievance.

> And Adam knew Eve his wife; and she conceived, and bare Cain, and said, I have gotten a man from the LORD. And she again bare his brother Abel. And Abel was a keeper of sheep, but Cain was a tiller of the ground. And

in process of time it came to pass, that Cain brought of the fruit of the ground an offering unto the LORD. And Abel, he also brought of the firstlings of his flock and of the fat thereof. And the LORD had respect unto Abel and to his offering: But unto Cain and to his offering he had not respect. And Cain was very wroth, and his countenance fell. And the LORD said unto Cain, Why art thou wroth? and why is thy countenance fallen? If thou doest well, shalt thou not be accepted and if thou doest not well, sin lieth at the door. And unto thee shall be his desire, and thou shalt rule over him. And Cain talked with Abel his brother: and it came to pass, when they were in the field, that Cain rose up against Abel his brother, and slew him.

—GENESIS 4:1–8

Counterattack: Ask God to remove the pain and grievance and to supply you with an abundance of forgiveness.

Retaliation

Retaliation is a weapon used to get back at you especially if you are making spiritual inroads in prayer and spiritual warfare. The more you war against the enemy, his desire to get back at you will increase. The Latin phrase for this is *quid pro quo*. You will advance on one hand, then the enemy will attempt to cause you to lose ground on the other. The ultimate intent is for you to lose control of your emotions, lose hope, and to break your focus. He may retaliate by hitting your finances, family, marriage, friendships, business, or any other area he feels will weaken you in your battle.

Then went Haman forth that day joyful and with a glad heart: but when Haman saw Mordecai in the king's gate, that he stood not up, nor moved for him, he was full of indignation against Mordecai. Nevertheless Haman refrained himself: and when he came home, he sent and called for his friends, and Zeresh his wife. And Haman told them of the glory of his riches, and the multitude of his children, and all the things wherein the king had promoted him, and how he had advanced him above the princes and servants of the king. Haman said moreover, Yea, Esther the queen did let no man come in with the king unto the banquet that she had prepared but myself; and to morrow am I invited unto her also with the king. Yet all this availeth me nothing, so long as I see Mordecai the Jew sitting at the king's gate. Then said Zeresh his wife and all his friends unto him, Let a gallows be made of fifty cubits high, and to morrow speak thou unto the king that Mordecai may be hanged thereon: then go thou in merrily with the king unto the banquet. And the thing pleased Haman; and he caused the gallows to be made.

—ESTHER 5:9–14

Counterattack: Decree and declare that no act of retaliation will prosper. Continue to reinforce your prayer shield and hedges of protection. Establish the Godhead as your Gatekeeper and Doorkeepers.

Sabotage

Sabotage is used to cause malicious destruction to an individual or the cessation of a work, a cause, and relationship or ministry. (For more details see *The Rules of Engagement, Vol. 2: Binding the Strongman*.)

> Now it came to pass, when Sanballat, and Tobiah, and Geshem the Arabian, and the rest of our enemies, heard that I had builded the wall, and that there was no breach left therein; (though at that time I had not set up the doors upon the gates;) That Sanballat and Geshem sent unto me, saying, Come, let us meet together in some one of the villages in the plain of Ono. But they thought to do me mischief. And I sent messengers unto them, saying, I am doing a great work, so that I cannot come down: why should the work cease, whilst I leave it, and come down to you? Yet they sent unto me four times after this sort; and I answered them after the same manner. Then sent Sanballat his servant unto me in like manner the fifth time with an open letter in his hand; Wherein was written, It is reported among the heathen, and Gashmu saith it, that thou and the Jews think to rebel: for which cause thou buildest the wall, that thou mayest be their king, according to these words.
>
> —NEHEMIAH 6:1–6

Counterattack: Bind and loose the spirit of Sanballat and Tobiah. Ask God to strengthen your hands as you work as unto the Lord. Ask God to supernaturally sustain you. Build prayer shields and hedges around your relationships, personhood, ministry, and business. Obliterate and annihilate satanic impressions, illusions, projections, perceptions, suggestions, suspicions, and deceptions set up as a decoy or an ambush to your soul and those assigned to pray with you, for you, on behalf of you, those that work with you, are assigned to you, and interact with you daily. (See Acts 13:50; 2 Thessalonians 2:1–10; 1 King 22:5–40.) Pray, "Father overthrow the plans of troublemakers, scorners, scoffers, mockers, persecutors, and character assassins. Expose satanic representatives and grant unto me divine strategies and tactics to identify, resist, and overcome plots and plans established for my demise. Amen." (See Psalm 5:10; 7:14–16; 34:21; 35:1–8; 52:5; 83:13–17; 141:10; Esther 9:25; Proverbs 26:27; 28:10; Daniel 3 and 6; Matthew 7:15–23; 2 Corinthians 11:14–15.)

Satanic Concentration

Satanic concentration is the total focus of satanic powers upon a specific object or person. Satan often focuses on one person in a family, a church, territory, or group of people to the exclusion of others. Usually this person has a divine purpose which threatens Satan. The following are examples of individuals who came under this attack. Read the references for further exposure and enlightenment.

- Joseph
  (Genesis 37:1–39:23)

- The nation of Israel
  (Exodus 1:1–12:51)

- Esther and Mordecai
  (Esther 1:1–8:17)

- Nehemiah
  (Nehemiah 4:1–23; 6:1–16)

- Jesus (the Gospels)

Counterattack: Pray that a prayer shield, the anointing, and bloodline form a hedge of protection which hides you from familiar spirits and all other demonic personalities making it difficult for them to effectively track or trace you in the realm of the Spirit. There shall be no perforations or penetrations.

Scandal

Everybody loves a juicy story, but some stories are just plain scandalous (pun intended). Take the story found in 1 Corinthians 5:1–5:

> It is reported commonly that there is fornication among you, and such fornication as is not so much as named among the Gentiles, that one should have his father's wife. And ye are puffed up, and have not rather mourned, that he that hath done this deed might be taken away from among you. For I verily, as absent in body, but present in spirit, have judged already, as though I were present, concerning him that hath so done this deed, In the name of our Lord Jesus Christ, when ye are gathered together, and my spirit, with the power of our Lord Jesus Christ, To deliver such an one unto Satan for the destruction of the flesh, that the spirit may be saved in the day of the Lord Jesus.

In this instance the scandal was the enemy's attempt to not only destroy that individual, but also to undermine the influence of the local assembly within its community as well. Jesus rebuked Peter because he perceived that Satan had set him up for a scandalous undertaking in His life.

> From that time forth began Jesus to shew unto his disciples, how that he must go unto Jerusalem, and suffer many things of the elders and chief priests and scribes, and be killed, and be raised again the third day. Then Peter took him, and began to rebuke him, saying, Be it far from thee, Lord: this shall not be unto thee. But he turned, and said unto Peter, Get thee behind me, Satan: thou art an offence unto me: for thou savourest not the things that be of God, but those that be of men.
>
> —Matthew 16:21–26

In this text, the word *offence* comes from the Greek word *skandalon*, and is probably a derivative of another Greek word *kampt* which is a trap-stick (bent sapling), or a snare (figurative cause of displeasure or sin), which gives occasion for someone to trip, stumble, or fall. Kampt is the actual feeling of being offended or the thing that causes the offense. Scandal is the English translation for this word. *The American Heritage Dictionary* defines this word as "a publicized incident that brings about disgrace or offends the moral sensibilities of society; a person, thing, or circumstance that causes or ought to cause disgrace or outrage." A scandal can cause irreversible damage to reputation or character, especially if there is a public disclosure of immoral or grossly improper behavior. Scandals cause shame, embarrassment, and disgrace. They can be caused by talk or expressions of injurious, malicious statements that are damaging to one's character.

The American Heritage Dictionary's definition of the word *scandal* is from a human perspective. Spiritually speaking, a scandal has a far more detrimental impact than just someone giving you a bad name, gossiping, or rehearsing an embarrassing, humiliating incident. Biblically and theologically speaking, a scandal is not just a weapon used to ensnare you; it is used to destroy your power, authority, and influence in both natural and spiritual realms and domains. According to Proverbs 22:1, "A good name is rather to be chosen than great riches, and loving favour rather than silver and gold."

Make certain your personal life is in order. Take care of the little foxes that can spoil the vine. (See Song of Solomon 2:15.)

Counterattack: Ask God to remove you from all appearance of evil and to forgive and cleanse you. Ask God to grant you the fruit of the Spirit and to wipe your image clean from the activities associated with the scandal and the residual effects in Jesus' name. Pray that God will vindicate your reputation and reengineer your character. Pray Psalm 51.

Seduction

This weapon is used just as bait is used for fish. It is designed to entice, attract, or draw a person into a wrong or foolish course of action. Seductions can be verbal or nonverbal.

> But they hearkened not: and Manasseh seduced them to do more evil than did the nations whom the LORD

destroyed before the children of Israel.

—2 KINGS 21:9

Because, even because they have seduced my people, saying, Peace; and there was no peace; and one built up a wall, and, lo, others daubed it with untempered morter.

—EZEKIEL 13:10

Now the spirit speaketh expressly, that in the latter times some shall depart from the faith, giving heed to seducing spirits, and doctrines of devils.

—1 TIMOTHY 4:1

Counterattack: Ask God to seduction-proof your spirit by giving you the gift of wisdom and discerning of spirits. Decree and declare that truth exposes error and that light dispels all darkness in Jesus' name.

Shame

The spirit of shame produces an internal feeling that we are somehow flawed as a person. It seduces people into believing that they are inadequate, bad, and no good. These feelings impede the maximization of potential and the fulfillment of purpose. In some people it can result in low self-esteem and a poor concept of self. Shame can involve family secrets, personal failures, and poor self-image. It can stem from issues like alcoholism, abuse, abortion, bankruptcy, unemployment, or divorce. This weapon is designed to erode the authenticity of who you really are: a person created in the image and likeness of God. Shame brings with it a sense of worthlessness, meaninglessness, depression, compulsive disorders, a deep sense of inferiority, inadequacy, alienation, helplessness, victimization, and isolation. Shame has led many people into living a life characterized by:

Self-abuse: either through condemning/belittling internal dialogue or with your body.

Abuse of others: taking out unresolved hurt and anger on others who are more helpless.

Chronic victimization: having no control over what happens, difficulties setting limitations with other people, difficulty in discerning and taking care of own personal needs, and difficulty in taking responsibility for own life.

Blaming: taking no ownership for what happens to them. Blaming others for what is happening or not happening in their life (mother, father, family, coworkers, the invisible "them," and "those people.")

Depression: feelings of hopelessness, helplessness, and powerlessness, and feeling overwhelmed by life itself.

Fear: of people, life, failure, success, opinions of others.

Control/manipulation: using ingenious schemes and manipulative ploys so as to feel as if they are in control in hopes that no one will see their emotional handicap. Bullying, being loud and boisterous.

Overachievement/perfectionism: doing things to make one "feel" good about themselves.

Suicide/attempts: attention-seeking activity, or feelings of "I don't want to live anymore."

And it came to pass after this, that Absalom the son of David had a fair sister, whose name was Tamar; and

Amnon the son of David loved her. And Amnon was so vexed, that he fell sick for his sister Tamar; for she was a virgin; and Amnon thought it hard for him to do any thing to her.... Howbeit he would not hearken unto her voice: but, being stronger than she, forced her, and lay with her. Then Amnon hated her exceedingly; so that the hatred wherewith he hated her was greater than the love wherewith he had loved her. And Amnon said unto her, Arise, be gone. And she said unto him, There is no cause: this evil in sending me away is greater than the other that thou didst unto me. But he would not hearken unto her. Then he called his servant that ministered unto him, and said, Put now this woman out from me, and bolt the door after her. And she had a garment of divers colours upon her: for with such robes were the king's daughters that were virgins apparelled. Then his servant brought her out, and bolted the door after her. And Tamar put ashes on her head, and rent her garment of divers colours that was on her, and laid her hand on her head, and went on crying. And Absalom her brother said unto her, Hath Amnon thy brother been with thee? but hold now thy peace, my sister: he is thy brother; regard not this thing. So Tamar remained desolate [isolated and alienated] in her brother Absalom's house.

—2 SAMUEL 13:1–2, 14–20

Counterattack: Pray Romans 8:26–29, "Likewise the Spirit also helpeth our infirmities: for we know not what we should pray for as we ought: but the Spirit itself maketh intercession for us with groanings which cannot be uttered. And he that searcheth the hearts knoweth what is the mind of the Spirit, because he maketh intercession for the saints according to the will of God. And we know that all things work together for good to them that love God, to them who are the called according to his purpose. For whom he did foreknow, he also did predestinate to be conformed to the image of his Son, that he might be the firstborn among many brethren." "Remember ye not the former things, neither consider the things of old. Behold, I will do a new thing; now it shall spring forth; shall ye not know it? I will even make a way in the wilderness, and rivers in the desert" (Isa. 43:18–19).

Sin

The Hebrew word for sin is *chattath*, from the root *chatta*, and in Greek it is *hamartia*. Both these words mean "to miss the mark." They are words that intimate something is off-target. As it relates to God's Law, they mean that one has failed to meet the standard or missed the targeted mark set by God for us. God's mark or standard is His Law. Therefore sin is the transgression of any of the laws of God. First John 3:4 offers the biblical definition of sin: "Whosoever committeth sin transgresseth also the law: for sin is the transgression of the law." Sin is the transgression of any of the laws of God.

Counterattack: Pray 1 John 1:9, "If we confess our sins, he is faithful and just to forgive us our sins, and to cleanse us from all unrighteousness."

Snares

In days of old snares were trapping devices. They primarily consisted of a noose and were used for capturing animals. In your life a snare is a satanic weapon that you should view as a source of danger or something that causes difficulty in escaping circumstances that are designed to cause your demise. Snares may come as a relationship or a habit-forming activities.

> And Saul said, I will give him her, that she may be a snare to him, and that the hand of the Philistines may be against him. Wherefore Saul said to David, Thou shalt this day be my son in law in the one of the twain. And Saul commanded his servants, saying, Commune with David secretly, and say, Behold, the king hath delight in thee, and all his servants love thee: now therefore be the king's son in law. And Saul's servants spake those words in the ears of David. And David said, seemeth it to you a light thing to be a king's son in law, seeing that I am a poor man, and lightly esteemed? And the servants of Saul told him, saying, On this manner spake David. And Saul said, Thus shall ye say to David, The king desireth not any dowry, but an hundred foreskins of the Philistines, to be avenged of the king's enemies. But Saul thought to make David fall by the hand of the Philistines.
>
> —1 SAMUEL 18:21–25

Counterattack: Pray Psalm 91:3, "Surely he shall deliver thee from the snare of the fowler, and from the noisome pestilence." Remember: "Foolish and unlearned questions avoid, knowing that they do gender strifes. And the servant of the Lord must not strive; but be gentle unto all men, apt to teach, patient, In meekness instructing those that oppose themselves; if God peradventure will give them repentance to the acknowledging of the truth; And that they may recover themselves out of the snare of the devil, who are taken captive by him at his will" (2 Tim. 2:23–26).

Spirits of Affinity

This spirit designs weapons that take a person into idolatry, causing them to lose favor with God. (Read *The Rules of Engagement, Vol. 2: Binding the Strongman* for more information and an indepth study of this spirit.) Exodus 20:2–3 states, "I am the LORD thy God, which have brought thee out of the land of Egypt, out of the house of bondage. Thou shalt have no other gods before me." This weapon was used in the life of many biblical characters such as King Solomon, Jehoshaphat, and the children of Israel.

> And Solomon made affinity with Pharaoh king of Egypt, and took Pharaoh's daughter, and brought her into the city of David, until he had made an end of building his own house, and the house of the LORD, and the wall of Jerusalem round about.
>
> —1 KINGS 3:1

> Now Jehoshaphat had riches and honour in abundance, and joined affinity with Ahab.
>
> —2 CHRONICLES 18:1

> Should we again break thy commandments, and join in affinity with the people of these abominations? wouldest not thou be angry with us till thou hadst consumed

us, so that there should be no remnant nor escaping?

—EZRA 9:14

Counterattack: Read Matthew 22:36–37, "Master, which is the great commandment in the law? Jesus said unto him, Thou shalt love the Lord thy God with all thy heart, and with all thy soul, and with all thy mind."

Spiritual Abortion

As in the natural, so it is in the spirit. The enemy seeks to apprehend and arrest wombs of the spirit in order to terminate that which is divine so that his plans and purpose can be manifested, thus superimposing them over the plans of God for your life.

And the serpent said unto the woman, Ye shall not surely die: For God doth know that in the day ye eat thereof, then your eyes shall be opened, and ye shall be as gods, knowing good and evil. And when the woman saw that the tree was good for food, and that it was pleasant to the eyes, and a tree to be desired to make one wise, she took of the fruit thereof, and did eat, and gave also unto her husband with her; and he did eat. And the eyes of them both were opened, and they knew that they were naked; and they sewed fig leaves together, and made themselves aprons....Unto the woman he said, I will greatly multiply thy sorrow and thy conception; in sorrow thou shalt bring forth children; and thy desire shall be to thy husband, and he shall rule over thee. And unto Adam he said, Because thou hast hearkened unto the voice of thy wife, and hast eaten of the tree, of which I commanded thee, saying, Thou shalt not eat of it: cursed is the ground for thy sake; in sorrow shalt thou eat of it all the days of thy life; Thorns also and thistles shall it bring forth to thee; and thou shalt eat the herb of the field; In the sweat of thy face shalt thou eat bread, till thou return unto the ground; for out of it wast thou taken: for dust thou art, and unto dust shalt thou return.

—GENESIS 3:4–7, 16–19

Counterattack: Bind the spirit of spiritual abortion. Decree and declare that everything that needs to be birthed through prayer and supplication will be birthed in its correct time and season. There will be no abortions and no stillbirths in Jesus' name.

Spiritual Miscarriage

Spontaneous, diabolically-initiated spiritual loss of divine purpose and destiny. This weapon was used effectively against Lot's wife:

And when the morning arose, then the angels hastened Lot, saying, Arise, take thy wife, and thy two daughters, which are here; lest thou be consumed in the iniquity of the city. And while he lingered, the men laid hold upon his hand, and upon the hand of his wife, and upon the hand of his two daughters; the LORD being merciful unto him: and they brought him forth, and set him without the city. And it came to pass, when they had brought them forth abroad, that he said, Escape for thy life; look not behind thee, neither stay thou in all the plain; escape to the mountain, lest thou be consumed. And Lot said unto them, Oh, not so, my Lord: Behold now, thy servant hath found grace in thy sight, and thou hast magnified thy mercy, which thou hast shewed unto me in saving my life; and I cannot escape to the mountain, lest some evil take me, and I die: Behold now, this city is near to flee unto, and it is a little one: Oh, let me escape thither, (is it not a little one?) and my soul shall live. And he said unto him, See, I have accepted thee concerning this thing also, that I will not overthrow this city, for the which thou hast spoken. Haste thee, escape thither; for I cannot do any thing till thou be come thither. Therefore the name of the city was called Zoar. The sun was risen upon the earth when Lot entered into Zoar. Then the LORD rained upon Sodom and upon Gomorrah brimstone and fire from the LORD out of heaven; And he overthrew those cities, and all the plain, and all the inhabitants of the cities, and that which grew upon the ground. But his wife looked back from behind him, and she became a pillar of salt.

—GENESIS 19:15–26

Counterattack: Decree and declare that your life is synchronized to God's original plan and purpose, and that there will be no miscarriage of anything God has planned for your life.

Stigmatization

This satanic weapon attempts to characterize or brand you as disgraceful or ignominious. It attaches "labels" upon a person, many of which are difficult to "shake off."

> But when the Pharisees heard it, they said, This fellow doth not cast out devils, but by Beelzeub the prince of the devils.

> —MATTHEW 12:24

Counterattack: Live your life in exact contrast to the stigma. Decree and declare that God is your defense.

Strongholds

A stronghold is a mental paradigm, ideology, heresy, information, doctrine, dogma, doctrines of men and devils, or any other mind-set Satan uses to control the destiny of an individual. He also uses strongholds to keep entire groups of people (communities, nations, kingdoms) in bondage. This powerful weapon blinds the minds and binds the will. He will use culture, fashion, music, political propaganda, religious and cultic activities, or anything else as a type of fortress hiding and camouflaging himself so as to go undetected by the masses.

> For the weapons of our warfare are not carnal, but mighty through God to the pulling down of strong holds.

> —2 CORINTHIANS 10:4

> Because that, when they knew God, they glorified him not as God, neither were thankful; but became vain in their imaginations, and their foolish heart was darkened.

> —ROMANS 1:21

Having the understanding darkened, being alienated from the life of God through the ignorance that is in them, because of the blindness of their heart.

—EPHESIANS 4:18

Counterattack: "For though we walk in the flesh, we do not war after the flesh: (For the weapons of our warfare are not carnal, but mighty through God to the pulling down of strong holds;) Casting down imaginations, and every high thing that exalteth itself against the knowledge of God, and bringing into captivity every thought to the obedience of Christ; And having in a readiness to revenge all disobedience, when your obedience is fulfilled" (2 Cor. 10:3–6). "The Lord is good, a strong hold in the day of trouble; and he knoweth them that trust in him" (Nah. 1:7).

Stumbling Blocks

Stumbling blocks are those things that obstruct movement and cause spiritual instability. In the original Hebrew text the word *mikashowl* had the connotation of an individual whose ankles could not support their weight, thus they would constantly stumble and fall.

Son of man, these men have set up their idols in their heart, and put the stumblingblock of their iniquity before their face: should I be enquired of at all by them? Therefore speak unto them, and say unto them, Thus saith the Lord GOD; Every man of the house of Israel that setteth up his idols in his heart, and putteth the stumblingblock of his iniquity before his face, and cometh to the prophet; I the LORD will answer him that cometh according to the multitude of his idols.

—EZEKIEL 14:3–4

But I have a few things against thee, because thou hast there them that hold the doctrine of Balaam, who taught Balac to cast a stumblingblock before the children of Israel, to eat things sacrificed unto idols, and to commit fornication.

—REVELATION 2:14

And a stone of stumbling, and a rock of offence, even to them which stumble at the word, being disobedient: whereunto also they were appointed.

—1 PETER 2:8

He that loveth his brother abideth in the light, and there is none occasion of stumbling in him.

—1 JOHN 2:10

Counterattack: Ask God to remove all stumbling blocks and to become the light to your pathway.

Suicidal Thoughts

Elijah is one of our greatest examples of the effectiveness of this weapon in the life of a believer. Even Jesus was attacked by this spirit. Just prior to His crucifixion, He was attacked in the garden of Gethsemane.

And Ahab told Jezebel all that Elijah had done, and withal how he had slain all the prophets with the sword. Then Jezebel sent a messenger unto Elijah, saying, So let the gods do to me, and more also, if I make not thy life as the life of one of them by to morrow about this time. And when he saw that, he arose, and went for his life, and came to Beersheba, which belongeth to Judah, and left his servant there. But he himself went a day's journey into the wilderness, and came and sat down under a juniper tree: and he requested for himself that he might die; and said, It is enough; now, O LORD, take away my life; for I am not better than my fathers.

—1 KINGS 19:1–4

Then saith he unto them, My soul is exceeding sorrowful, even unto death: tarry ye here, and watch with me.

—MATTHEW 26:38

Counterattack: "Thou wilt keep him in perfect peace, whose mind is stayed on thee: because he trusteth in thee" (Isa. 26:3). "And the peace of God, which passeth all understanding, shall keep your hearts and minds through Christ Jesus" (Phil. 4:7).

Thorn in the Flesh

A thorn in the flesh is an area of weakness that Satan is allowed to consistently focus on so that as a result of the existence of the thorn the individual, like Paul, fosters a total dependence on God and not self.

And lest I should be exalted above measure through the abundance of the revelations, there was given to me a thorn in the flesh, the messenger of Satan to buffet me, lest I should be exalted above measure.

—2 CORINTHIANS 12:7

Counterattack: Build prayer shields, firewalls around your life. Decree and declare according to Psalm 89:21–23, "With whom my hand shall be established: mine arm also shall strengthen him. The enemy shall not exact upon him; nor the son of wickedness afflict him. And I will beat down his foes before his face, and plague them that hate him." I am strengthened by the arm of the Lord. The enemy shall not exact himself against me. Father, weed out all who oppose me and hate me. Do not allow evil to come nigh to my dwelling. You are my hiding place. I dwell in the secret place of the most high God.

Traditions of Men

Traditions are elements of a culture passed down from generation to generation, especially by oral communication and modeling.

> Why do thy disciples transgress the tradition of the elders? for they wash not their hands when they eat bread. But he answered and said unto them, Why do ye also transgress the commandment of God by your tradition?
>
> —Matthew 15:2–3

> And honour not his father or his mother, he shall be free. Thus have ye made the commandment of God of none effect by your tradition.
>
> —Matthew 15:6

> For the Pharisees, and all the Jews, except they wash their hands oft, eat not, holding the tradition of the elders.
>
> —Mark 7:3

Counterattack: Decree and declare that the kingdom of heaven reigns and rules over the affairs of man.

Transference of Spirits

Transference of spirits is the transmigration of a spirit from one person to another. This can happen by any of the following:

- Laying on of hands
- Association
- Sexual encounters
- Incantation
- Contracts
- Covenants
- Oaths
- Talisman

Be not deceived: evil communications corrupt good manners.

—1 Corinthians 15:33

Counterattack: Study *The Rules of Engagement, Vol. 2: Binding the Strongman*. Bind and loose any spirit that has been transferred in Jesus' name. Command them to loose their hold.

Unbelief

Unbelief is another powerful weapon. It differs from doubt in that doubt says, "I need more information." Unbelief, on the other hand, says "No matter how much information you give me, I still don't believe." The first generation of Hebrews who were delivered from the hand of Pharaoh died because of their unbelief. This weapon restrains the power of God.

> And he did not many mighty works there because of their unbelief.
>
> —Matthew 13:58

> Let us therefore fear, lest, a promise being left us of entering into his rest, any of you should seem to come short of it. For unto us was the gospel preached, as well as unto them: but the word preached did not profit them, not being mixed with faith in them that heard it....Let us labour therefore to enter into that rest, lest any man fall after the same example of unbelief.
>
> —Hebrews 4:1–2, 11

Counterattack: Decree and declare that the spirit of unbelief is superimposed by the Spirit of faith.

Uncleanness

Moral, psychological, physical, or environmental defilement.

> And there was in their synagogue a man with an unclean spirit; and he cried out....And when the unclean spirit had torn him, and cried with a loud voice, he came out of him. And they were all amazed, insomuch that they questioned among themselves, saying, What thing is this? what new doctrine is this? for with authority commandeth he even the

unclean spirits, and they do obey him.

—MARK 1:23, 26–27

Counterattack: Decree and declare that the environment, spirit, or mind of a person is purified and cleansed by the blood, by the Spirit, and by the Word of the Lord. Command every unclean spirit to leave in the name of Jesus. Decree and declare that the former occupied space is swept clean in Jesus' name.

Underachievement

This powerful intrinsic weapon is used by a demotivating spirit, driving a paradigm which will cause you to:

- Avoid success-related activities

- Doubt your ability

- Assume success is related to luck, education, money, "who you know," or to other factors out of your control. Thus, even when successful it isn't as rewarding to the unmotivated person because they doesn't feel responsible or it doesn't increase his/her pride and confidence.

- Quit when having difficulty because you believe failure is caused by a lack of ability which you "obviously don't have."

- Choose tasks that are not challenging, passion- or purpose-driven.

- Work with little drive or enthusiasm because outcome isn't thought to be related to effort.

Counterattack: Bind the spirit of underachievement. Decree and declare that through Christ you can fulfill purpose, maximize potential, and bring glory to the name of the Lord. Set the bar of achievement higher.

Unforgiveness

Unforgiveness is the refusal to release someone from an offense or wrongdoing. Unforgiveness grieves the Holy Spirit and is sometimes one of the most difficult sins to confess and to get over because we so often think we must feel it emotionally when we forgive someone. The very act of forgiveness is an act of our will and not our emotions. If unforgiveness is left to fester it has the potential to give rise to bitterness. Characteristics of unforgiveness include: anger, hurt, resentfulness, replaying an event or words spoken, or vengeance. As long as an act of wrongdoing or the assailant remains in your thoughts, you have not forgiven. Sometimes you have to forgive yourself, too. Don't grieve the Spirit by holding onto things too long. Cast your cares on the Lord. Forgiving means leaving everything in God's hands, recalling that ultimately vengeance is His.

> And when ye stand praying, forgive, if ye have ought against any: that your Father also which is in heaven may forgive you your trespasses. But if ye do not forgive, neither will your Father which is in heaven forgive your trespasses.
>
> —Mark 11:25–26

Counterattack: "For if ye forgive men their trespasses, your heavenly Father will also forgive you: But if ye forgive not men their trespasses, neither will your Father forgive your trespasses" (Matt. 6:14–15).

Unholy Alliances

Ungodly, close associations established through demonic influences so as to reinforce satanic plans and purposes in your life.

> Also I in the first year of Darius the Mede, even I, stood to confirm and to strengthen him. And now will I shew thee the truth. Behold, there shall stand up yet three kings in Persia; and the fourth shall be far richer than they all: and by his strength through his riches he shall stir up all against the realm of Grecia. And a mighty king shall stand up, that shall rule with great dominion, and do according to his will. And when he shall stand up, his kingdom shall be broken, and shall be divided toward the four winds of heaven; and not to his posterity, nor according to his dominion which he ruled: for his kingdom shall be plucked up, even for others beside those. And the king of the south shall be strong, and one of his princes; and he shall be strong above him, and have dominion; his dominion shall be a great dominion. And in the end of years they shall join themselves together; for the king's daughter of the south shall come to the king of the north to make an agreement: but she shall not retain the power of the arm; neither shall he stand, nor his arm: but she shall be given up, and they that brought her, and he that begat her, and he that strengthened her in these times.
>
> —Daniel 11:1–6

Counterattack: Ask God to assist you in discerning the spirits of those that operate around you. Bind every spirit that is diabolically assigned to you and decree and declare that no weapon formed against you shall prosper.

Unsanctified Souls

Although many believers are truly and sincerely saved, their souls remain unconverted. The following are examples of some of the areas we need to ask God to cleanse and purify:

- Agendas: a cause of action

- Ambitions: a strong desire for achievement or success

- Appetites: an instinctive physical desire

- Desires: longings, wishes

- Ideologies: the body of ideas reflecting the social needs and aspirations of an individual

- Intentions: an aim that guides action and objectives

- Motives: an emotion, desire, physiological need, impulse, purpose, aim

- Passions: powerful emotions such as love, joy, hatred, or anger

- Perceptions: recognition and interpretation of sensory stimuli based chiefly on memory

- Philosophies: thought about thoughts

And the Lord said, Simon, Simon, behold, Satan hath desired to have you, that he may sift you as wheat: But I have prayed for thee, that thy faith fail not: and when thou art converted, strengthen thy brethren.

—LUKE 22:31–32

Counterattack: Pray the following passages, "Behold, thou desirest truth in the inward parts: and in the hidden part thou shalt make me to know wisdom. Purge me with hyssop, and I shall be clean: wash me, and I shall be whiter than snow. Make me to hear joy and gladness; that the bones which thou hast broken may rejoice. Hide thy face from my sins, and blot out all mine iniquities. Create in me a clean heart, O God; and renew a right spirit within me. Cast me not away from thy presence; and take not thy holy spirit from me" (Ps. 51:6–11); "Wherefore lay apart all filthiness and superfluity of naughtiness, and receive with meekness the engrafted word, which is able to save your souls" (James 1:21).

Vain Imagination

Narcissism and arrogance of the mind often lead believers into more dependence on self, education, good looks, intelligence, or the likes, than dependence on God. This is a trick of the enemy because without God we are nothing.

And the LORD smelled a sweet savour; and the LORD said in his heart, I will not again curse the ground any more for man's sake; for the imagination of man's heart is evil from his youth; neither will I again smite any more every thing living, as I have done.

—GENESIS 8:21

And it come to pass, when he heareth the words of this curse, that he bless himself in his heart, saying, I shall have peace, though I walk in the imagination of mine heart, to add drunkenness to thirst.

—DEUTERONOMY 29:19

And it shall come to pass, when many evils and troubles are befallen them, that this song shall testify against them as a witness; for it shall not be forgotten out of the mouths of their seed: for I know their imagination which they go about, even now, before I have brought them into the land which I sware.

—DEUTERONOMY 31:21

Counterattack: Pray verses 4 through 6 of 2 Corinthians 10, "For the weapons of our warfare are not carnal, but mighty through God to the pulling down of strong holds; casting down imaginations, and every high thing that exalteth itself against the knowledge of God, and bringing into captivity every thought to the obedience of Christ; and having in a readiness to revenge all disobedience, when your obedience is fulfilled."

Vengeance/Vindictiveness

Getting back at and getting even with someone are two acts of revenge. Getting revenge should never be on the tongue of a believer. There are universal, spiritual laws that work for us if we are wronged. Besides, God reminds us that vengeance belongs to Him, and that He will repay any wrongdoing. So remember the next time you are tempted by the enemy to get someone back, Romans 12:19 states:

> Dearly beloved, avenge not yourselves, but rather give place unto wrath: for it is written, Vengeance is mine; I will repay, saith the Lord.

Truly, it is a dangerous thing to fall into the hands of an angry God!

Counterattack: Pray Hebrews 10:30, "For we know him that hath said, Vengeance belongeth unto me, I will recompense, saith the Lord. And again, The Lord shall judge his people." This is no light matter. God has warned us that He will hold as to account. God will judge His people. Nobody is getting by with anything, believe me. Let God be God!

Vexations

The enemy will attempt to overwhelm, harass, and exasperate you—don't let him. This is not your battle; the battle belongs to the Lord. Go into prayer and spiritual warfare against this spirit. Insist that it cease and desist in the name of the Lord.

> Better is an handful with quietness, than both the hands full with travail and vexation of spirit.
> —ECCLESIASTES 4:6

Now about that time Herod the king stretched forth his hands to vex certain of the church.

—Acts 12:1

Counterattack: Pray *The Rules of Engagement, Vol. 1: The Art of Strategic Prayer and Spiritual Warfare.*

Violence

In this text violence is likened to wine, which inebriates and causes a person to lose reason. Violence is hideous because it does not take into consideration laws, personhood, personal possessions, property, or the right to live.

The Lord trieth the righteous: but the wicked and him that loveth violence his soul hateth.

—Psalm 11:5

Therefore pride compasseth them about as a chain; violence covereth them as a garment.

—Psalm 73:6

For they eat the bread of wickedness, and drink the wine of violence.

—Proverbs 4:17

Counterattack: Bind the spirit of violence and decree and declare that peace, collaboration, justice, and reconciliation replace violence. Pray *The Rules of Engagement, Vol. 1: The Art of Strategic Prayer and Spiritual Warfare.*

Wars/Conflicts

War is the state of open, armed, and prolonged conflict between nations, organizations, and people. The enemy loves to keep things stirring and in motion in order to derail, distract, and destroy. Satan employs demonic spirits to create discord and disharmony in your relationships, especially with those who have a divine assignment. In an attempt to camouflage your real foe, he will attempt to blind you spiritually and emotionally by causing you to focus on the person or situation he uses, rather than the spirit that is behind the conflict. Remember, no matter who or what he uses he is the culprit behind every conflict and battle.

> For, when we were come into Macedonia, our flesh had no rest, but we were troubled on every side; without were fightings, within were fears.
>
> —2 Corinthians 7:5

> From whence come wars and fightings among you? come they not hence, even of your lusts that war in your members?
>
> —James 4:1

Counterattack: Pray the following exhaustive list of Scripture passages:

> Thou wilt keep him in perfect peace, whose mind is stayed on thee: because he trusteth in thee.
>
> —Isaiah 26:3

> Lord, thou wilt ordain peace for us: for thou also hast wrought all our works in us.
>
> —Isaiah 26:12

For unto us a child is born, unto us a son is given: and the government shall be upon his shoulder: and his name shall be called Wonderful, Counsellor, The mighty God, The everlasting Father, The Prince of Peace. Of the increase of his government and peace there shall be no end, upon the throne of David, and upon his kingdom, to order it, and to establish it with judgment and with justice from henceforth even for ever. The zeal of the Lord of hosts will perform this.

—Isaiah 9:6–7

And seek the peace of the city whither I have caused you to be carried away captives, and pray unto the Lord for it: for in the peace thereof shall ye have peace.

—Jeremiah 29:7

For I know the thoughts that I think toward you, saith the Lord, thoughts of peace, and not of evil, to give you an expected end.

—Jeremiah 29:11

Pray for the peace of Jerusalem: they shall prosper that love thee.

—Psalm 122:6

And all thy children shall be taught of the Lord; and great shall be the peace of thy children.

—Isaiah 54:13

And the peace of God, which passeth all understanding, shall keep your hearts and minds through Christ Jesus.

—Philippians 4:7

And let the peace of God rule in your hearts, to the which also ye are called in one body; and be ye thankful.

—COLOSSIANS 3:15

And the fruit of righteousness is sown in peace of them that make peace.

—JAMES 3:18

Weights

Weights are satanic burdens. They can come in a variety of shapes and forms, such as emotional weights, which can be yours or someone else's, financial weights, or psychological weights. They are worries, cares, or concerns intended to keep you earthbound.

A false balance is abomination to the LORD: but a just weight is his delight.

—PROVERBS 11:1

Counterattack: Pray this verse from Hebrews, "Wherefore seeing we also are compassed about with so great a cloud of witnesses, let us lay aside every weight, and the sin which doth so easily beset us, and let us run with patience the race that is set before us."

Works of the Flesh

The works of the flesh are carnally-motivated activities and self-seeking endeavors which keep an individual from living a kingdom-oriented lifestyle.

Now the works of the flesh are manifest, which are these; Adultery, fornication, uncleanness, lasciviousness, Idolatry, witchcraft, hatred, variance, emulations, wrath, strife, seditions, heresies, Envyings, murders, drunkenness, revellings, and such like: of the which I tell you before, as I have also told you in time past, that they which do such things shall not inherit the kingdom of God.

—Galatians 5:19–21

Counterattack: Pray Galatians 5:18–21, "Why don't you choose to be led by the Spirit and so escape the erratic compulsions of a law-dominated existence? It is obvious what kind of life develops out of trying to get your own way all the time: repetitive, loveless, cheap sex; a stinking accumulation of mental and emotional garbage; frenzied and joyless grabs for happiness; trinket gods; magic-show religion; paranoid loneliness; cutthroat competition; all-consuming-yet-never-satisfied wants; a brutal temper; an impotence to love or be loved; divided homes and divided lives; small-minded and lopsided pursuits; the vicious habit of depersonalizing everyone into a rival; uncontrolled and uncontrollable addictions; ugly parodies of community. I could go on. This isn't the first time I have warned you, you know. If you use your freedom this way, you will not inherit God's kingdom" (MSG).

Worldliness

According to 1 John 2:16, worldliness is characterized by the lust of the flesh, the lust of the eyes, and the pride of life (see *The Rules of Engagement, Vol. 2: Binding the*

Strongman and *The Prayer Journal* for more details on this subject). John's statement contrasts itself with things that are in God as opposed to being in the world. When a person looks for enjoyment, success, and the fulfillment of purpose outside of the will of God, this is worldliness. It is like building your house on sand as opposed to a firm foundation. When emotional, economic, relational, or spiritual storms come, a worldly person has nothing of substance on which to weather the storms. Worldliness to a Christian amounts to foolishness because even though you may gain carnal things, your gain will be at the expense of your soul.

> For what shall it profit a man, if he shall gain the whole world, and lose his own soul?

> —MARK 8:36

Counterattack: "Love not the world, neither the things that are in the world" (1 John 2:15).

Worry

Worry is an apprehensive or distressed state of mind. Jesus gives us much insight into the futility of worry especially in light of our alternative: faith and believing in our heavenly Father as *Jehovah Jireh,* the provider and the giver and sustainer of life. Worry cannot change anything but your physical and mental well-being. Worry is a contributing factor of high blood pressure, insomnia, anxiety, and a whole host of other conditions. Remember, don't pray if you are going to worry, and don't worry if you are going to pray.

Which of you by taking thought can add one cubit unto his stature? And why take ye thought for raiment? Consider the lilies of the field, how they grow; they toil not, neither do they spin: And yet I say unto you, That even Solomon in all his glory was not arrayed like one of these. Wherefore, if God so clothe the grass of the field, which to day is, and to morrow is cast into the oven, shall he not much more clothe you, O ye of little faith? Therefore take no thought, saying, What shall we eat? or, What shall we drink? or, Wherewithal shall we be clothed? (For after all these things do the Gentiles seek:) for your heavenly Father knoweth that ye have need of all these things. But seek ye first the kingdom of God, and his righteousness; and all these things shall be added unto you. Take therefore no thought for the morrow: for the morrow shall take thought for the things of itself. Sufficient unto the day is the evil thereof.

—Matthew 6:27–34

Counterattack: "Trust in the Lord with all thine heart; and lean not unto thine own understanding. In all thy ways acknowledge him, and he shall direct thy paths" (Prov. 3:5–6). Decree and declare that your God shall supply all your need according to His riches in glory.

Yokes

In biblical days a yoke was a crossbar with two U-shaped pieces that encircle the necks of a pair of oxen or other draft animals working together. One animal would be the leader, the other the follower. If the follower attempted to go in another direction, the lead animal would redirect it by jerking its neck. The jerk would cause discomfort and even pain. This activity was undertaken not only to increase productivity, but also to tame and train less domesticated animals. Likewise with Satan, he will attempt to yoke you to a spirit whose assignment is to lead you into a direction away from God and the fulfillment of purpose. Yokes are Satan's way of derailing you and altering your destiny. Being yoked to the enemy removes your freedom of choice, but being yoked to Christ restores it. He states in Matthew 11:29–30, "Take my yoke upon you, [an invitation for you to use your freedom of choice to make a decision] and learn of me; for I am meek and lowly in heart: and ye shall find rest unto your souls; for my yoke is easy, and my burden is light."

> And it shall come to pass in that day, that his burden shall be taken away from off thy shoulder, and his yoke from off thy neck, and the yoke shall be destroyed because of the anointing.
>
> —Isaiah 10:27

> That I will break the Assyrian in my land, and upon my mountains tread him under foot: then shall his yoke depart from off them, and his burden depart from off their shoulders.
>
> —Isaiah 14:25

> Stand fast therefore in the liberty wherewith Christ hath made us free, and be not entangled again with the yoke of bondage.
>
> —Galatians 5:1

Counterattack: Ask God to remove the predilection to go against His will. Ask Him to grant you discipline, consistency, and a love for His Word. Decree and declare that yokes are broken and burdens are lifted by reason of the anointing in Jesus' name.

Conclusion

ISAIAH 54:17 AND Revelation 12:11 are two of the most comforting verses in the Bible. They should empower you to know that although you cannot always prohibit Satan from forming weapons against you: "No weapon that is formed against thee shall prosper; and every tongue that shall rise against thee in judgment thou shalt condemn. This is the heritage of the servants of the LORD, and their righteousness is of me, saith the LORD" (Isa. 54:17), and you will overcome every attack "by the blood of the Lamb, and by the word of their [your] testimony" (Rev. 12:11). The Lamb has already done His part in shedding His blood—now do yours by declaring and continuously testifying: no weapon formed against me shall prosper!

This book should be used in conjunction with *The Rules of Engagement, Vol. 2: Binding the Strongman,* and *The Prayer Journal.* These books combined will give you strategies and tactics to render these weapons ineffective.

Notes

Anger

1. *Strong's Greek and Hebrew Dictionary* (Nashville, TN: Crusade Bible Publishers, 1980).

Enmeshment

1. Salvador Minuchin, MD, *Psychosomatic Families: Anorexia Nervosa in Context* (Cambridge, MA: Harvard University Press, 1978).

2. Melody Beattie, *Codependent No More* (Center City, MN: Hazelden, 1986).

Indifference

1. Web site: http://netherlands.usembassy.gov/memorial_day_2004.html (accessed March 1, 2006).

Miseducation

1. Web site: www.thememoryhole.org/edu/school-mission (accessed March 1, 2006).

OTHER MATERIALS
BY DR. N. CINDY TRIMM

To supplement your prayers and extend your prayer time, these messages are available in tape, CD, book, or bookmark form:

The Rules of Engagement, Volume I: The Art of Strategic Prayer and Spiritual Warfare

The Rules of Engagement, Volume II: Binding the Strongman

The Prayer Journal

The Rules of Engagement, Volume IV: The Weapons of Our Warfare
(scheduled release: 2006)

The Rules of Engagement, Volume V: The Spirit of the Watchman

The Rules of Engagement, Volume VI: Using the Names of God

The Rules of Engagement, Volume VII: The Power of the Anointing
(scheduled release: 2006)

Who I Am in Christ

What I Believe the Lord For

The Battle Cry of a Warrior

Millennium Creed

Names of Jesus

Names of the Holy Spirit

Prayers for the Saints

ABOUT THE AUTHOR

For over twenty-five years this dynamic, multigifted world changer has been equipping people to fulfill their destinies and maximize their potential. Highly respected by persons from all walks of life, a teacher of teachers, preacher, coach, mentor, consultant, author, and former government senator, Dr. N. Cindy Trimm reaches into the depths of her existence, draws on knowledge, experience, and wisdom, and pours out unselfishly into the lives of others.

A much sought-after speaker, founder, and CEO of a network of companies and ministries, Dr. Trimm has traveled extensively throughout North and South America, Europe, the Caribbean, and Africa. Her unique style is permeated with intellectually compelling commentary, revolutionary insights, and contemporary practical applications.

She has received numerous honors and distinctions, including awards from the Queen of England, the Duke of Edinburgh, and the Governor of Bermuda. Dr. Trimm is listed among the Five Hundred Leaders of Influence, 2000 Notable American Women, The International Who's Who of Professional and Business Women; receiving citations as Outstanding Christian Woman of the Year, Woman of the Year for Outstanding Community and Professional Achievement, and the 20th Century Award for Achievement.

A highly respected success coach and prosperity mentor to civic and spiritual leaders, indeed a leader of leaders, she emphatically states, "All these things that I once thought very worthwhile now I've cast aside so that I can put my trust and hope in Christ alone. Everything else is worthless when compared with the priceless gain in knowing Christ Jesus as my Lord."

For information on bookings or
to place an order:

Cindy Trimm Corporation
P.O. Box 101240
Ft. Lauderdale, FL 33311

www.cindytrimm.com

Phone: (954) 933-9191
Fax: (954) 934-0188
E-mail: infor@cindytrimm.com